THE HISTORY

OF THE

LAW OF PRESCRIPTION IN ENGLAND.

THE HISTORY

OF

THE LAW OF PRESCRIPTION
IN ENGLAND.

BEING THE YORKE PRIZE ESSAY OF THE UNIVERSITY OF
CAMBRIDGE FOR 1890.

BY

THOMAS ARNOLD HERBERT, B.A., LL.B.,

OF THE INNER TEMPLE, BARRISTER AT LAW; LATE EXHIBITIONER AND SCHOLAR,
AND McMAHON LAW SCHOLAR OF ST JOHN'S COLLEGE, CAMBRIDGE:
EQUITY SCHOLAR OF THE INNER TEMPLE, 1889.

LONDON:

C. J. CLAY AND SONS,

CAMBRIDGE UNIVERSITY PRESS WAREHOUSE,

AVE MARIA LANE.

1891

CAMBRIDGE UNIVERSITY PRESS
Cambridge, New York, Melbourne, Madrid, Cape Town,
Singapore, São Paulo, Delhi, Mexico City

Cambridge University Press
The Edinburgh Building, Cambridge CB2 8RU, UK

Published in the United States of America by Cambridge University Press, New York

www.cambridge.org
Information on this title: www.cambridge.org/9781107665651

First published 1891
First paperback edition 2013

A catalogue record for this publication is available from the British Library

ISBN 978-1-107-66565-1 Paperback

TO

HERBERT HARDY COZENS-HARDY, Esq., Q.C., M.P.

AS A SMALL TOKEN

OF ADMIRATION AND GRATITUDE,

THIS BOOK

IS BY KIND PERMISSION

DEDICATED

BY THE AUTHOR.

PREFACE.

THE Yorke Prize in the University of Cambridge is offered annually for the best essay upon some branch of the Law of Property in various countries. This was the successful essay for 1890. The essay as sent in comprised a history of Limitation, since that is included in Prescription in the wider sense in which it is used by some writers. But, as I have explained, I do not consider that it properly is Prescription. This view is shared by the examiners, and that part has with their assent been omitted.

There is no book definitely upon Prescription in English Law; the information has to be collected from the various sources where it lies hid. The books I have found most useful have been Brooke's, Rolle's, Bacon's and Viner's Abridgments, Comyn's and Cruise's Digests, Coke upon Littleton and the Institutes, and the notes and references to the Year-books and reports therein contained. Two branches of the subject have been fully and ably dealt with by modern writers: that of Commons by Mr Joshua Williams, and that of Easements by Messrs Gale and Goddard in their well-known books. Accordingly, though it was necessary, for the sake of completeness, to say something about both Commons and Easements, I have treated both those subjects in a most cursory manner. But I have in both cases examined the original authorities for myself; and upon several points I have ventured to differ from Mr Goddard. I have followed the plan of quoting largely from the reports of cases partly because in many instances the subject-matter, or the mode of expression, has been of an interest sufficient to justify me, and partly because in expounding a legal principle a more accurate notion is generally conveyed by quoting the expressions of judges of eminence than by attempting to give the effect of decisions in words of one's own. The work has had to be done in a rather scrappy manner, with often short spells and long intervals. But I venture to hope that the various parts are sufficiently connected to make an intelligible whole.

T. A. H.

7 NEW SQUARE,
  LINCOLN'S INN,
     1891.

CONTENTS.

H.   *b*

CHAPTER VIII.

CHAPTER IX.

CHAPTER X.

CHAPTER XI.

TABLE OF CASES.

INTRODUCTORY.

THE history of the Law of Prescription in England is a subject of no small complexity. It is desirable therefore to start upon our inquiry with notions as clear and definite as the nature of the case allows. First, then, as to the derivation and meaning of the word Prescription. A Praescriptio appears to have been the earliest kind of exceptio used in the Roman formulary system of actions[1]; or rather, strictly speaking, it was the parent form from one use of which the exceptio sprang. "Praescriptio, quae vox a Graecis hominibus in Latinae linguae consuetudinem inducta est—παραγραφή enim a Graecis dicitur quae a Latinis praescriptio, et παραγράφειν praescribere—id est excipere." Franc. Hotoman. *Quaest.* 2. 6. "Est ergo praescriptio omnis exceptio essentiam capiens ex tempore." Rogerus de Praescrip. *Tract.* XVII. p. 48. "Usucapio L. 12 Tab. inducta est, praescriptio jure Praetorio—illa directum dominium adjicit—haec non dominium quod a Praetore dari non potest sed exceptionem ex aequitate suppeditat." Perezii *Praelect.* in Lib. 7 c. tit. 33.

It was as the name denotes placed at the beginning of the formula to limit the scope of the inquiry. As used by the plaintiff its purpose was to restrict the action to claims already due, that the decision might be without prejudice to future claims; but its chief use was as a defence introduced by the Praetors to supply the deficiencies of usucapio. Usucapio was available only to those who had the Commercium[2] and did

---

[1] Sandars, *Just.* LXVII. seq.   [2] Code, 7. 39. 8. Dig. 8. 5. 10.

not apply to provincial lands. The Praetors, on the analogy of usucapio, introduced a praescriptio applying to provincial lands, wherein the plea of possessio longi or longissimi temporis was raised. The effect of a praescriptio of long possession was the same as that of usucapio, it was not a mere plea of a Statute of Limitation, but gave a right against third parties[1]. Justinian (*Inst.* II. 6, Sandars, p. 22, seq.) entirely altered the scope of usucapio and longi temporis praescriptio. Usucapio was, under his system, the name used in connexion with movables wherever situated; the old longi temporis praescriptio was made to apply to all lands wherever situated, and the name praescriptio no longer denoted merely a part of the formula, indeed it no longer existed as part of the formula, but attained the meaning it has in England at the present time. But to say that it attained its present meaning is to be anything but definite; for it is hard to ascertain if it has in English Law any one meaning, and if so what that is. The cause of this is that none of those who have written upon prescription have been at any pains to make clear at the outset what meaning they attach to the term, but have left that to be gathered here and there throughout their writings. It is true that Coke, *Inst.* 113 b, gives us the definition " praescriptio est titulus ex usu et tempore substantiam capiens ab auctoritate legis;" but this still leaves open the question whether negative prescription or limitation is in his view to be accounted prescription. For Prescription we are told[2] is of two kinds, positive or acquisitive, or negative, restrictive, or a limitation of actions.

But if negative prescription is included in prescription, then Coke and Blackstone are clearly wrong in saying that there cannot be prescription of land. And to take almost at haphazard a few passages out of well-known writers, we find the most apparently contradictory statements. Thus Williams on *Commons*, p. 2, says, " A title by prescription can only be made to incorporeal hereditaments. A man cannot by prescription make a title to land...." On the other hand Wharton

---

[1] Here Ortolan seems mistaken in saying usucapio is positive, prescriptio negative: Hunter, *Roman Law*, p. 143.

[2] Austin, *Jurisp.* Wharton, *L. Lex.* s. v. Digby, *Hist. R. P.* p. 149.

(*Law Lexicon*, 80) says, "There are two kinds of prescription, viz.:—(1) Negative, which relates to realty or corporeal hereditaments, whereby an uninterrupted possession for a given time gives the occupier a valid and unassailable title by defeating all claimants of every stale right and deferred litigation, now mainly governed by 3 and 4 Will. IV. c. 27 (The R. P. Limitation Act); and (2) positive, which relate to incorporeal hereditaments and originated at Common Law, from immemorial or long usage only."

Again, Austin does not quite agree with either of the foregoing. After dividing prescription into positive or acquisitive and negative or restrictive, he says (*Jurisp.* Vol. I. pp. 509 to 516), "In other words acquisitive prescription is unknown to the English Law in its direct form. Directly and avowedly length of enjoyment is not a mode of acquisition or (in the language of our own law) a title. But a grant is a title directly and avowedly: and by feigning a grant from length of enjoyment, length of enjoyment becomes a title in effect, or that mode of acquisition which is styled acquisitive prescription is introduced indirectly."

It is true that he afterwards (p. 526) modifies this. "I also stated this too roundly that acquisitive prescription in its direct form is unknown to the English Law. A prescription in a que estate as it is called, or a prescription of an easement appurtenant is recognised directly by the English Law. But I think this is the only instance. Easements in gross are not acquired by prescription in that direct way, but in the oblique mode before explained. Rights amounting to proprietas or dominium are never acquired by direct prescription. The operation of the different Statutes of Limitation is purely negative or extinctive."

Perhaps we may find some explanation of the use of the word in English Law by again looking to the Roman Law. The term Praescriptio is a term of Roman Law, and it must have been introduced into English Law with some reference to its use in that Law. Now we find that in Roman Law, according to the history of the word before explained, praescriptio had no application to movables—so in English Law

1—2

there is not a single instance of the term being applied to movables. But if Limitation is prescription then it would seem that movables ought to have been prescribable for. And the real explanation may be here—the plea of prescription was in Roman Law *in form* a plea of a Statute of Limitation—prescriptio est exceptio temporis ratione—but in *fact* it gave a title against third parties—differing therefore from a Statute of Limitation, which in general, though the Act now in force in England is somewhat different, may bar the remedy of one person after a certain time; but in itself gives no further right to the person setting it up.

Markby, in his *Elements of Law*, has some interesting remarks upon the effect of time in various systems of Law in fortifying titles. "Sometimes it is laid down, plainly and simply, that a person, who has been for a certain time in possession, shall be considered as owner. Sometimes without professing in express terms to recognise the person in possession, as owner, all means of asserting his ownership are taken away from any other claimant who has been for a certain time out of possession." § 381.

"It is a remarkable instance of the shifting use of language that the word 'prescription' has been used, sometimes exclusively in reference to one of these distinct forms; sometimes exclusively in reference to the other; sometimes in reference to both." He distinguishes Limitation from Prescription; but he makes prescription apply to Land. In this, I think, he is mistaken, as will appear later. § 382.

Again, the inclusion of Limitation in Prescription may easily have arisen in the minds of the less clear thinkers from the treatment of both in 'that profitable and necessary statute' 32 Hen. VIII. c. 2.—That statute, which will be treated of a little later on, in its application to writs of right is a Statute of Limitations—in its application to prescription, merely has the effect of shortening the time for which prescription must be proved—but the different effect in the two cases is very easily lost sight of.

So then Prescription proper as treated by Coke and Blackstone is distinct from Limitation and does not apply to corporeal hereditaments. This, I think, is undoubtedly the correct view, and though it has sometimes been contended that 3 and 4 Will. IV. c. 27 (the Real Property Limitation Act) has the effect of a positive prescription, yet this is now determined not to be so. Dart. *V. and P.* 6th Ed. p. 463 : see *Wilkes v. Greenway, Times*, May 30th, 1890. Accordingly though the subject of Limitation is one of much intricacy and interest I do not deal with it further, as I do not consider that it comes properly within the scope of my subject.

Another point must be noted here for the sake of clearness, though it will be treated more in detail later on ; and that is the nature of the right of prescription. In the first place a prescription which is a personal must be distinguished from a custom which is a local or general usage. It is personal in the sense that it can only be claimed by a man as having belonged to himself and his ancestors, or to a man and those whose estate he has ; which is called a prescription in a que estate.

Again, not every enjoyment would support a prescription. It must have been an actual user, without interruption or license from those against whom it was sought to be maintained. It must have been such a right as could be granted, since every prescription presumed a grant ; and it must have been such an user as was reasonable at the time when the grant was alleged to have been made. Suffice it to mention these matters here since convenience requires that I should first examine the length of time required to establish a right, assuming it to be of a kind that could properly be prescribed for.

CHAPTER I.

For what time Prescription must run.

By the Common Law a man might show his title to what he claimed by proving that he and his ancestors, or that he and those whose estate he has, enjoyed it from time[1] immemorial. As Littleton saith 170, "And note that no custom is to bee allowed but such custom as hath bin used by title of prescription, which is all one in the law. For some have said that time out of minde should be said from time of limitation in a writ of right, that is to say from the time of King Rich. I. after the conquest as is given by the Stat. of West. I......And insomuch that it is given by the said estatute that in a writ of right none shall be heard to demand of the seisin of his ancestors of longer time than of the time of King Rich^d. aforesaid, therefore this is proved that continuance of possession or other customs and usages used after the same time is the title of prescription. And this is certain, and others have said that well and truth it is that seisin and continuance after the limitation is a title of prescription as is aforesaid and by the cause aforesaid. But they have sayd that there is also another title of prescription that was at the Common Law before any estatute of limitation of writs, and that it was where a custom or usage or other thing hath been used for time whereof mind of man runneth not to the contrary......and insomuch that such title of prescription

---

[1] Bracton, lib. 2, c. 22. 10, 51 b. 'Qualiter acquiritur possessio per usu-captionem. Usucaptio i.e. sine titulo et traditione per longam continuam et pacificam possessionem ex diuturno tempore.' So again 'per longam et pacificam seisinam, habitam per patientiam et negligentiam veri domini.' So 'omnes actiones in mundo infra certa tempora habent limitationem."

was at the Common Law and not put out by an estatute, ergo it abideth as it was at the Common Law."

Littleton here says that the time of prescription is the time of legal memory which had finally been fixed at the first year of Richard I.; but that some alleged that there was also the other time of memory which had existed at the Common Law prior to the imposition of any limitation in writs of right, and that a prescription might be pleaded for this longer period. It is possible that the longer prescription arising by the Common Law may have continued, but it is to be observed that the prescription going back to the time of legal memory was the construction of the Courts of the old time of prescription, *i.e.* the mind of man was irrebuttably presumed not to run to the contrary after the time of legal memory; and one fails to see what advantages anyone could have got by claiming under the longer prescription. It is not like claiming a thing by Common Law prescription in addition to the Prescription Act which gives additional advantages; but nobody could have gained by a claim of user for time whereof the mind of man did not run to the contrary anything that he could not have gained by a like claim under the construction that the mind of man did not run to the contrary after the time of legal memory. It is certainly impossible to find an instance of any such claim, and it is safe to conclude that although it may have theoretically existed, yet that being of no practical use it fell into desuetude.

Now the time of legal memory was no doubt originally the same as the time of actual memory; but it was found convenient to have some time fixed beyond which memory could be presumed not to go. This period was made to depend on the period fixed for limiting the bringing a writ of right. This was a fluctuating period dating from some historical event. Thus "in ancient time the limitation in a writ of right was from the time of Henry I. whereof it was said a tempore regis Henrici senioris[1]. After that by the Statute of Merton the limitation was from the time of Henry II.; and by the Statute of Westminster I. the limitation was from the time of Rich. I.,

[1] Co. Litt. 144 b. *Regist.* 158. Bracton, fo. 373. 5. *Ass.* p. 2. 34 Hen. VIII. 40.

and this is that limitation that Littleton speaketh of, whereof
in the *Mirror*[1] in reproof of the law it is thus said, "Abusion est
de counter cy longe temps, dount nul ne poet testmoigner de
vieu et de oyer, que ne dure my generalement ouster 40 ans."

And the time of limitation was at other times[2] fixed at
other periods. But the beginning of the reign of Rich. I. was
the final period, and still remains the limit of the period of legal
memory.

As to this in the specimen of the writ in Glanvil I. 13, ca. 3
(Beames), "The King to the Sheriff health. If G. the son of
J. shall make you secure of prosecuting his claim then summon
by good summoners twelve free and lawful men of the neighbour-
hood of such a vill, that they be before me or my justices on
such a day prepared on their oath to return if J. the father
of the aforesaid G. was seised in his demesne as of fee of one
yardland in that vill on the day of his death if he died after
my first coronation (20th Oct. 1154, Co. 2 *Inst.* 94), and if the
said E. be his nearer heir. And in the mean time let them
view the land and cause their names to be imbreviated; and
summon by good summoners R. who holds that land that he
be then there to hear such recognition and have there the
summoners, &c. witness, &c." But if the ancestor was seised
in the manner before mentioned and had begun a voyage then
the writ will be in a somewhat different form. *Ibid.* ca. 4.

The first year of the reign of Rich. I. remained without
change the time of limitation in writs and the time from which
prescription had to run until the alteration made by "a profitable and necessary Statute made anno 32 Hen. VIII. (c. 2)[3].
By that Act the former limitation of time in a writ of right is
changed and reduced to threescore years next before the teste
of the writ, and so of other actions as by the Statute at law
appeareth."

The Statute after reciting the evils that arise from want of
some period of limitation provides that no manner of person or
persons shall from henceforth sue, have or maintain any writ of
right, or make any *prescription*, Title or Claim of to or for any

---

[1] *Mirror*, ca. 5. 11.   [2] Blackst. 31 n.

[3] Co. Litt. 115 a.

Manors, Lands, Tenements, Rents, Annuities, Commons, Pensions, Portions, Corrodies, or other hereditaments of the possession of his or their ancestor or predecessor and declare and allege any further seisin or possession of his or their ancestor or predecessor, but only of the seisin or possession of his ancestor or predecessor which hath been or now is or shall be seised of the said Manors, Lands, Tenements, Rents, Annuities, Commons, Pensions, Portions, Corrodies or other hereditaments within threescore years next before the teste of the same writ or next before the said *prescription*, Title or Claim so hereafter to be sued, commenced, brought, made or had.

Sec. II.   Limits a period of 50 years next preceding the teste of the writ in any action possessory.

Sec. III.   Limits a period of 30 years preceding the teste of the writ in any action upon a man's own seisin.

Sec. IV.   Limits a period of 50 years in any avowry or cognisance for any rent, suit or service.

Sec. V.   Enacts that all formedons in Reverter, formedons in remainder, and scire facias as on fines shall be sued within 50 years next after the title and cause of action fallen.

Sec. VI.   Enacts that if any person suing in any of the said actions or suits or making avowry, cognisance, *prescription* or claim, cannot prove that he or his ancestors or predecessors were in actual seisin or possession within the times limited, if the same be traversed, they and their heirs shall be utterly barred.

Sec. VII.   A saving for all suits depending in 1546.

Sec. VIII.   Provides for all the disabilities of infancy, coverture, imprisonment, absence out of the realm giving a further period of six years from the removal of the disability.

Sec. IX.   Extends to the heirs of any person under the above disabilities the six years' grace, to begin from the death of the ancestor under such disability.

Sec. X.   Provides that in case any suit depending in 1546 shall abate by the death of any of the parties, the other parties or the heir of the deceased party may for one year have the same privilege of pursuing their remedy as was granted to suits actually depending.

Sec. XI.   Provides that if any false verdict be given in any of the above proceedings the party grieved may bring his attaint, and upon succeeding therein may recover, anything to the contrary in the Act notwithstanding.

Now upon this Act it is to be observed "that it extendeth not to a formedon in the discenders." This appears to be a casus omissus: for Sec. V. refers to a formedon in remainder and reverter. And in *Fitzwilliam's case* (Dyer 278) where it was argued that a formedon in the discender was included in the clause of the Statute relative to writs of right, it was held by three judges, one doubting, that a formedon was not strictly a writ of right, and that it was not therefore anywhere hit by the Statute.

This defect was not remedied until 21 Jac. I. c. 16, which requires formedons of every kind to be brought within 20 years after the descent of the title.

Nor to pursue Coke does the Statute extend (Co. Litt. 115 a) " to the services of escuage homage or fealty for a man may live above the time limited by the Act. Neither doth it extend to any other service which by common possibility may not happen or become due within 60 years as to cover the hall of the lord or to attend on his lord when he goeth to warre or the like: nor when the seisin is not traversable or issuable, because the statute refers entirely to seisin and therefore cannot extend to a case where seisin does not become the subject of trial[1]. Neither doth it extend to a rent created by deed nor to a rent reserved upon any particular estate, for in the one case the deed is the title and in the other the reservation; nor to any writ of right of advowson, quare impedit, or assise of darrein presentment (for there was a parson of one of my churches that had been incumbent there above 50 yeares and dyed but lately) or any writ of right of ward or ravishment of ward, &c., but they are left as they were before the Statute 32 Hen. VIII. c. 2." Until Mar. Parl. 2, cap. 5, it was doubtful whether the several writs here mentioned in respect to advowsons and wardships were within the Statute, but the late Statute declared that 32 Hen. VIII. c. 2 did not extend to them. But by 7 Anne, c. 18, it is enacted with regard to advowsons that no usurpation shall

[1] Co. 10 and 11. *Bevil's Case. Sir W. Foster's Case*, 8 Co. 65.

displace the estate of the patron and he may present on the next avoidance as if there had been no usurpation.

Now the effect of the Statute 32 Hen. VIII. c. 2 with regard to those claims that fell within it, and in particular with regard to prescription, was this : it made it necessary in any claim by prescription, to give evidence of seisin either by the claimant himself, or his ancestors, or those whose estate he had as the case might be, within the 60 years next preceding the date of the teste of the writ[1]. It did not make a prescription of 60 years all that was required, for after the statute a claim by prescription might be defeated by showing that it first arose subsequent to the first year of Richard I. but it prevented the assertion of stale claims which had begun before the time of legal memory, but the enjoyment of which had been suspended for more than the 60 years. Its effect was purely that of a statute of limitation upon the assertion of prescriptive claims.

It is only right to admit that some writers came to consider that this statute did not affect prescription at all. They treat it as applying a new principle which might, by analogy, have been extended to prescription, but which in fact was not. I cannot help thinking that it had the effect here stated. It expressly mentions prescription, and that certainly in the sense, or in a sense which includes the sense, in which I use the word. The point is not of much importance because there would seldom be a case where a right which had not been enjoyed in some way or other for 60 years would be attempted to be established, or if attempted would not be found to have been abandoned.

Before this it had been provided by 4 Hen. VII. c. 24 (the Statute of Fines) with regard to a fine with proclamations that all persons having present rights of entry and not being under disabilities should be barred by a fine with proclamations in five years from the last proclamation : and that persons under disabilities should be barred in five years from the removal of the disabilities. It also barred all persons not having present

---

[1] See *Bevil's Case*, 4 Rep. 8, where it was held that the statute does not include the case of a service that may by common possibility not be required within 60 years.

rights of entry in five years after they obtained a present right of entry unless under disability, and then within five years from the removal of the disability. *And the Statute 4 and 5 Anne,* c. 16, provided that no claim or entry to avoid a fine with proclamations is sufficient unless an action be commenced within one year after, and prosecuted with effect.

In order therefore to succeed in a claim to a prescriptive right under the Act of 32 Hen. VIII. c. 2, it was necessary to give evidence of enjoyment within the last 60 years for about 30 years. *Bailey v. Appleyard,* 8 A. and E. 161. The time does not seem to have been exactly fixed. Thus evidence of long user, if other circumstances were unfavourable, was insufficient (2 Saund. 175); while enjoyment for a shorter period supported by other evidence would do. *Bailey v. Shaw,* 6 East, 215. But at any rate after 21 Jac. I. c. 16, it was fixed by analogy to the period required by that statute at 20 years[1].

That evidence then made a prima facie case and the onus was thrown on the party disputing the prescription of showing that it had been first enjoyed since the year 1189. If this could be done the prescription was defeated[2]. Every prescription presumed a grant[3]; and a prescription could only be made of a right which could have been granted; but if no evidence that the enjoyment began subsequent to 1189 were given it was not necessary to give any positive evidence of an actual grant[4].

Despite this presumption in aid of prescription a claimant could not feel safe unless he could prove his right so far back as 1189; and it often came about that a claim was defeated by showing, *e.g.* that no grant could have been legally made, or that the right must have been extinguished by unity of possession since 1189; or even that it was extremely improbable that a grant was ever made[5]. For the purpose of avoiding the necessity of diving into such ancient history a presumption

[1] *Mounsey v. Ismay*, 34 L. J. Ex. p. 55. *Gaved v. Martyn*, 34 L. J. C. P. 356. *Hollins v. Verney*, 13 Q. B. D. 314. *Lowe v. Carpenter*, 6 Ex. 825. *Carr v. Foster*, 3 Q. B. 585.

[2] *Jenkin v. Harvey*, 1 Cr. M. and R.

at p. 894.

[3] *Potter v. North*, Vent. 397. *Pelham v. Pickersgill*, 1 J. R. 667.

[4] *Berry v. Pope*, Cro. Eliz. 118.

[5] See 1st Report of R. P. Commis. p. 51.

of a modern lost grant was introduced by the Courts in aid of prescription, and after proof of enjoyment by the person claiming for 20 years. The effect of this was that after proof of enjoyment for 20 years the jury was told that they might presume a grant immediately before the 20 years which had been lost, and no proof therefore that the right had been first enjoyed at any time between 1189 and the beginning of the 20 years would avail to defeat a claim of this kind. So that now the claimant was only bound to be prepared with evidence of enjoyment for 20 years, which might have been the 20 years next preceding the action, and must of course have been within the 60 years preceding action. The practice does not appear to have been uniform with regard to the weight to be given to the evidence of 20 years' enjoyment. Some judges, and this appears the better opinion, merely held that it was cogent evidence from which the jury were authorised to find a modern lost grant, others seem to have regarded it as an irrebuttable presumption of law that there was a modern lost grant after proof of 20 years' enjoyment. Of course if after proof of 20 years' user the presumption was an irrebuttable one, then evidence to show that no grant had actually been made would have been inadmissible. And it seems to have been thought that the fact that in so few cases rebutting evidence was called that the presumption was one juris et de jure. It appears at first sight strange that in all cases, at any rate in which the person supposed to have made the grant was living, he should not have been called to swear that he made no grant. But this is explained by the fact that until 1851 parties to actions were not competent witnesses, and they were only made so in that year by 14 and 15 Vic. c. 99.

From a careful reading of the cases (see in particular *Dalton v. Angus,* 3 Q. B. D. 85, 4 Q. B. D. 162; 6 App. Cas. 740) I suggest that the truth is that the introduction of the theory was a fiction introduced to satisfy the early technicality of the Common Law. It was no doubt a piece of bold judicial legislation, which by the way all legal fictions are in a greater or less degree.

But so also had been the gradual lessening by the judges

of the length of time over which evidence of user was required
for a claim by prescription; and both had no doubt been made
in obedience to a general feeling that where a right had been
enjoyed as of right for 20 years or thereabouts, the owner
should be quieted in such enjoyment by some means or other.
I suggest that then as in the course of time Law became less
technical, as it undoubtedly did and continues to do, the idea
of the actual grant became of less importance, except of course
as limiting the class of rights that could be claimed by requiring that the right must have been such an one as could
have been granted, and that the principle of the Prescription
Act, which appears so new and certainly is new so far as any
definite formulation of it is concerned, viz. that of a right from
enjoyment for a fixed period founded on no presumption of any
longer usage, or of any actual grant, was in reality anticipated.
It seems then that in the case of a claim by lost grant, the
parties could not be called to prove whether a grant had actually been made or not, but that evidence was admissible to
show that no grant could have been made, as *e.g.* owing to the
disability of the supposed grantor; or that no grant was actually made in this sense, viz. that the presumption of a grant
was made rather as the result of an estoppel by conduct when
the supposed grantor had been in for 20 years with the acquiescence of the grantor, not being under a disability; but
that evidence was admissible to show that no grant had been
made, *i.e.* that the presumption ought not to be raised, by
explaining the supposed acquiescence, and showing that the
possession of the supposed grantee was by the licence, or without the knowledge of the grantor. In such case it would be
for the jury to find as a fact whether the grant had been
made. Though when the 20 years' possession was proved, and
there was no evidence on the other side, the jury was directed to find that a grant had been made. The point is put
very clearly in the judgment of Brett, L. J. in his judgment
in *Dalton v. Angus* in the Court of Appeal, 4 Q. B. D. at
p. 200. He there says, "This then being the doctrine which
is to be applied, a question has been raised whether in applying it it is necessary to find formally that there has been a

grant which is lost, or whether it is sufficient to find the fact of an uninterrupted user of 20 years after knowledge of the burden imposed on the adjacent land without going on to find the inference that there has been a grant and that it has been lost. That must depend on whether the inference is to be treated as a necessary legal consequence or as an inference of fact. If it is an inference merely of law, I can see no distinction, not even the slightest, between the doctrine or application of the doctrine of a lost grant and the doctrine of prescription under the Prescription Act. If we were to hold that it is a mere inference of law, it seems to me that we should be doing in an analogous form precisely what was done by the judgment of Mr Justice Lush, which I think cannot be supported. In order therefore to support such a claim the existence of a lost grant must be found as a fact. This raises another question, viz. whether the Judge may under certain circumstances direct the jury as matter of law to find the fact; and if he may, what are the circumstances under which he may do so? It is admitted by everyone, I think, that he is bound to do so when there is evidence of 20 years' uninterrupted user with knowledge of the facts and no other evidence. Now arises another question, which is, what other evidence is admissible or may be acted upon? Is it only evidence of acts of interruption? or although no act of interruption has been done may evidence be given tending to show that no grant in fact was ever made? If the parties are alive may they be called to prove conclusively that there never was a grant? If the question whether there ever was a grant is one of fact to be found by the jury I know of no principle of Law which can exclude evidence tending to show that there never was in fact such a grant."

Now, in the view that I take, the only difference between the claim by lost grant and under the Act, was one of detail. The principle was the same—the Prescription Act only made a difference in fixing a legislative instead of a judicial limit to the time required for proof of possession—in fixing the further periods after which possession was indefeasible—in requiring the possession to have been before action brought without interruption acquiesced in for a year, which had the peculiar consequence hereinafter alluded to, and in the definite provision made in the case of light, in which case the leave or acquiescence must be evidenced by a written document.

This presumption however was a fiction, and as such was not regarded with great favour. At any rate it was only resorted to in cases when the evidence was not sufficient to support a prescription, *e.g.* in cases where the user could have been shown to have begun later than 1189.

So in *Bright v. Walker*, 1 Cr. M. and R. 217, it is said, " such presumption did not always proceed on a belief that the thing presumed had actually taken place, but as is properly said by Mr Starkie in his excellent treatise on evidence, a technical efficacy was given to the evidence of possession beyond its simple and natural force and operation, and though in theory it was presumptive evidence in practice and effect it was a bar."

There seems, however, to have been this difference between the evidence of the 20 years' user required to support a claim of prescription by the presumption that it had been enjoyed from time immemorial, and that which supported a claim by lost grant, that in the latter case the evidence should have been directed to show that the usage began about the time of the supposed grant[1].

A prescriptive right might be claimed alternatively on the ground given from time immemorial, and of modern lost grant, and the same evidence of user might have sufficed for both, but it would appear that the claimant could succeed only on one of these grounds, since evidence which was framed to prove the beginning of the right 20 years or more before action brought would apparently exclude the presumption that it had been enjoyed from time immemorial, and if on the other hand the evidence were claimed as raising a presumption that the user had been from time immemorial, the presumption of a modern grant was excluded.

Markby, *Elements of Law*, §§ 415, 416, 417 objects to Prescription as understood in English Law being founded on a

---

[1] Per Paterson, J. in *Blewitt v. Tregonning*, 3 Ad. and El. at p. 585.

presumed grant. But he does not seem fully to appreciate the manner in which it is so founded. According to him the theory of grant must either recognise a justus titulus, in which case a protest by the servient owner would negative the right; or it must be that the Law, in spite of all, violently presumes what never took place, in which case a protest would rather strengthen the prescription.

But it is not immaterial to point out that if the grant was supposed before 1189 no protest now could make any difference; while if the grant supposed be a modern one, in our law the grant would not be found by the jury, if the enjoyment had been contested. The truth is that the theory of grant squares with neither of Markby's alternatives. It operates rather as an estoppel by conduct which is not raised unless the enjoyment has been such that justice requires the establishment of the right. This view will be abundantly illustrated in treating of the requirements of enjoyment at Common Law, and under the Act.

A curious point arose with regard to the inconsistency of a modern grant with a claim by prescription, in the case of *Addington v. Clode and others*, 2 Black. 989, though in that case the grant had not been pleaded. It was an action of trespass by Addington against the Defendant for breaking and entering his close at Upottery. The Defendant pleaded as owner of lands at Upottery, a prescriptive right of common for all commonable cattle levant and couchant. At the trial the Defendant produced two ancient grants undated. One was a grant of the lands then in possession of the Defendant to his predecessors in title; and by the other Henry de la Pomereye confirmed to such predecessors the said lands, and in the same deed was contained the following grant :—

"And I will and grant for me and my heirs that the said William (the predecessor of the Defendant) his heirs and assigns shall have with his beasts common pasture on my mountain of Uppoteri." The judge then pointed out that this grant was inconsistent with the plea of prescription, and verdict was entered for the Plaintiff. But afterwards the Defendant moved for a new trial on the ground that the

H. 2

grant might have only been in confirmation of an antecedent prescription and so was not necessarily inconsistent with it. And it was held that the grant being undated might have been before the time of legal memory, or might have been only in confirmation of a prior prescription, and in either way not inconsistent. It was therefore a question for the jury to decide whether either of these suppositions were true, and since it had not been left to them a new trial was granted.

Thus far of Prescription at Common Law. The Policy of the Law all along, from the successive alterations of the period for the commencement of legal memory, and the "profitable and necessary Statute" of Henry VIII. down to the later doctrine of the Courts that after evidence of user for a comparatively short time the presumption arose of a grant lost immediately before that time, had been to shorten the time required for the establishment of the right. It had now come to be the case that evidence of user for twenty or thirty years was all that in most cases was required to raise the presumption of prescription from the time of legal memory, rebuttable no doubt by evidence of commencement since that date. But the presumption of a modern lost grant after such user was not so defeasible. It was however a fiction, and was felt in many cases to be a burdensome one, since juries did not understand or like to find as a fact that a grant had been made, when they felt perfectly sure that no such thing had taken place. It was therefore felt to be time to put the law in this matter upon a more satisfactory and logical basis; the outcome of this feeling was the Prescription Act of 1832, 2 and 3 Will. IV. c. 71. As was said by Martin, B., in *Mounsey v. Ismay*, 3 H. and C. 486,

"The occasion of the enactment of the Prescription Act is well-known. It had long been established that the enjoyment of an easement as of right for twenty years was practically conclusive of a right from the reign of Richard I., or in other words of a right by Prescription, except proof was given of an impossibility of the existence of a right from that period: and a very common mode of defeating such a right was proof of a unity of possession since the time of legal memory. To meet this the grant by lost deed was invented, but in progress of time a difficulty arose in requiring a jury to find upon their oaths that a deed had been executed which everyone knew never existed : hence the Prescription Act." This Act made a considerable alteration in the mode by which a prescription might be claimed, with definite provisions as to what length of time rendered a right indefeasible. But it must be borne in mind that the Act was only supplementary to the Common Law right. It took away no right already existing, but merely gave a new mode of asserting such right if desired. It is still possible and usual to claim a right alternatively under the Prescription Act and at the Common Law. And such alternative claim is more beneficial than the old alternative claim of enjoyment time out of mind, and under the doctrine of a modern lost grant, since it was alternative in the sense of being concurrent and subsidiary rather than exclusive. Under the old claim it was necessary to choose under which to proceed, since the evidence which supported one defeated the other ; whereas a claim which may fail to come within the words of the Prescription Act may by the same evidence be shown to be a good claim under the Common Law. But it is still of course necessary in availing oneself of the claim under the Common Law to choose whether one will claim as by enjoyment from the time of legal memory or under a lost grant. There are thus three grounds of stating one's claim. See *Bailey v. Stevens*, 31 L. J., C. P., 226.

1. Under the Prescription Act. Failing that :—

2. Under the Common Law, in which case one must choose whether to claim

(A) By enjoyment from the time of legal memory, or

(B) By reason of a lost grant.

The question of the presumption of a modern grant which had been lost was much discussed in the important case of *Dalton v. Angus*, 3 Q. B. D. 85, in the Court of Appeal, 4 Q. B. D. 162, and in the *House of Lords*, 6 App. Cas. 740.

In that case the question arose whether a house which had enjoyed support from adjacent land for 20 years had thereby acquired such a right to support as to give an action for damages to the owner when such support was removed. The question was very fully considered, and the opinions of the judges were delivered in the House of Lords. The effect of the decision in the House of Lords is not so precisely given as that in the Court of Appeal, but it was substantially to affirm that decision. I think that the effect of the decision may be stated thus: The right of lateral support for a building from adjacent land is an easement which may be acquired by prescription from the time of legal memory or by grant express or implied, or perhaps under the Prescription Act. It is also a right which may be acquired, after 20 years' uninterrupted enjoyment, though proved not to have existed before the beginning of the 20 years, if the owner of the adjacent land must have known it was being enjoyed and was capable at that time of making a grant, and after 20 years of such enjoyment the right will not be defeated by showing that no grant was in fact made. It is true that many of the Judges who delivered their opinions to the House of Lords considered that as applied to the right to support the presumption of a lost grant was unreasonable. But that was upon the ground that it was a negative easement: that all the acts of the person claiming the right were done upon his own land, so that the servient owner had no means of preventing them, and that as therefore he could not have been held to have acquiesced in them, no grant ought to be presumed against him. This of course does not in the least affect the principles of the presumption in the cases of claims in the nature of positive easements.

But, as Mr Goddard, *Easements,* p. 150, points out, the theory is peculiar. He there says, "When the theory of this doctrine is considered it will readily be seen how contrary to reason it is to say that when a house has stood for 20 years it shall or may be presumed that the owner of the adjoining land has made a grant of a right to support which everybody knows full well he has not made, and that a jury sworn to find a verdict according to the evidence shall be obliged to find or may if they think fit find as a fact that which they know has never happened: that they shall be obliged to find this if the house has stood for 20 years, just the reverse if it has only stood for nineteen and a half years."

It must not be forgotten at the same time that the presumption of a lost grant is only in aid of a claim by prescription, and that it is inapplicable and cannot be claimed in any case in which the claim could not be made by prescription. Thus in *Bryant v. Lefever*, 4 C. P. D. 172, a claim was made to an uninterrupted flow of air over the whole of adjacent property, but it was held that this was a claim which could not be prescribed for, and that therefore it could not be claimed by a presumption of lost grant. But the right to passage of air through a defined channel may be claimed by lost grant. *Bass v. Gregory*, 25 Q. B. D. 481.

CHAPTER II.

THE PRESCRIPTION ACT.

To come now to the provision of the Prescription Act in detail. The first section provides:—

"Whereas the expression 'Time immemorial or time whereof the memory of man runneth not to the contrary' is now by the Law of England in many cases considered to include and denote the whole period of time from the reign of King Richard the First whereby the title to matters that have been long enjoyed is sometimes defeated by showing the commencement of such enjoyment, which is in many cases productive of inconvenience and injustice, for remedy thereof be it enacted by the King's most excellent Majesty, by and with the advice and consent of the Lords Spiritual and temporal and Commons in the present Parliament assembled and by the authority of the same that no claim which may be lawfully made at the common law by custom prescription or grant to any right of common or other profit or benefit to be taken and enjoyed from or upon any land of our Sovereign Lord the King his heirs or successors or any land being parcel of the Duchy of Lancaster or the Duchy of Cornwall or of any ecclesiastical or lay person or body corporate except such matters and things as are herein specially provided for and except tithes rent and services shall where such right profit or benefit shall have been actually taken and enjoyed by any person claiming right thereto without interruption for the full period of thirty years be defeated or destroyed by showing only that such right profit or benefit was first taken or enjoyed at any time prior to such period of thirty years but nevertheless such claim may be defeated in any other way by which the same is now liable to be defeated, and when such right profit or benefit shall have been so taken and enjoyed as aforesaid for the full period of sixty years the right thereto shall be deemed absolute and indefeasible unless it shall appear that the same was taken and enjoyed by some consent or agreement expressly made or given for that purpose by deed or writing."

This first section deals solely with rights of common and other profits a prendre. There seems to be no particular reason why the periods in this case should have been fixed at 30 and 60 years except the feeling that the period should be rather longer in cases where the actual produce of the land was taken. It must be observed that any length of enjoyment short of 60 years gives only a title defeasible by any means before allowed; after 60 years the only mode of defeating the title is a consent or agreement by deed or writing. Now up to the completion of the 60 years the right is defeasible in any way in which it might have been defeated at Common Law. The rights therefore that can be gained under this section are only rights known to the Common Law. That is prescription under this section is like prescription at Common Law, obliged to be consistent with a supposed grant. So that no right can be gained under the Act which could not have been granted. Thus where the right is directly contrary to a Statute, or to an existing prescriptive right; or where the enjoyment has been against a person who did not know of the user, or who was incapable of resisting by reasonable means, or where the dominant or servient owners are of such a class as to be incapable of taking by or making a grant, in all these cases, which will be dealt with more in detail in their proper places, no right could be gained under the Act. It must be observed, however, that after the period of 60 years, in respect of rights coming under the first section, and of 40 years in the case of rights under the other sections, and of 20 years in claims to light under the third section, the Statute provides that the

rights are to be indefeasible in any save the specified ways. Hence after these respective periods the rights in question no longer depend upon the possibility of grant, but are, by the positive enactment of the Statute, constituted absolute rights quite independent of the Common Law. Now upon this point I venture to think that Mr Goddard, whose admirable book upon *Easements* is worthy of the most careful attention, has taken the wrong view of the construction of the Act as interpreted by the cases. What he says is that where a right is made absolute by the Statute it depends solely upon the Statute and cannot be claimed at Common Law. He draws this inference from the words of Lord Westbury in his judgment in a case of *Tapling v. Jones*, 11 H. L. C. 290, as follows:—
"The right to an ancient light depends upon positive enactment: that it is matter juris positivi, and does not require and therefore ought not to be rested on any presumption of grant or fiction of a license having been obtained from the adjoining proprietor." Goddard, p. 194. It is true that was a case in which only a right to light was in question. But it is obvious that all rights made indefeasible by the Act must be treated in the same way, and they are so treated by Mr Goddard himself, p. 213, p. 194—5.

But as I understand the judgment of Lord Westbury it was delivered with reference merely to claims under the Act and really afforded no ground for the assumption that claims under the Common Law were excluded. It must be admitted that the words of Lord Cranworth at p. 310 give some colour to the assumption. He says, "The right to enjoy light through a window looking on a neighbour's land, on whatever foundation it might have rested previously to the passing of the 2 and 3 Will. IV. c. 71, depends now on the provisions of that Statute." It is quite true that these words may be read to mean that the right depends upon the Statute alone. But it is also true that they may be read as saying that the right, on whatever foundation it rested before the Act, now rests *in addition* upon the Statute; and that is the way in which I think they should be read. If it were not so the law would be the same as to other rights coming within the Act so soon as, by the lapse of the periods of 40 or 60 years as the case might be, they became absolute and indefeasible. The result of that would be that so soon as the 40 or 60 years had passed the character of the right would be entirely changed, not only in this respect in which it undoubtedly is changed, that it is indefeasible, and does not depend on any theory of grant; but also that it could not be claimed at Common Law, but only under the Act. I cannot find that this has ever been contended, and Mr Goddard himself does not so treat the Act. It is of course always a question whether any particular right is within the Act. It was not intended to create any new kind of right. Its scope is less extensive than Common Law prescription. It certainly may be said that no right that could not have been claimed (I do not say established) at Common Law before the Act can be claimed under the Act. Hence as no right that was incapable of grant could have been prescribed for at Common Law, that still remains a primary restriction under the Act with the single exception of light. It is quite true that the Act is of a highly technical character, and that it is apparently so carelessly drawn that some provisions are inconsistent with others, and that there is the greatest difficulty in discovering what the real intention of the legislature was. But as the only ground for saying that light is claimable only under the Act is that it is made an absolute right, all absolute rights under the Act should be on the same footing. This question has not been free from judicial comment since the decision in *Tapling v. Jones.* In two cases, both as good fortune would have it cases of light, *Tapling v. Jones* was quoted to the Court, and it was necessary for the decision, to say whether that case had interpreted the Act as taking away the right to prescribe at Common Law. In both cases it was held that it had not. Mr Goddard's way of dealing with those cases is somewhat summary; he says they are wrong, p. 261.

The first of them is *Lanfranchi v. Mackenzie*, L. R. 4 Eq. 426. Malins, V. C., there says, " Mr Glasse has referred me to a case of *Jones v. Tapling*, and has argued that it now depends not on the Common Law, or the ancient principle, but upon the Statute. I do not understand the Statute to have made any difference. I only read the Statute as meaning this (and I believe it has been uniformly so read) that there was no absolute period theretofore, but now the period is fixed at twenty years."

Now, so far as some part of that passage goes, there is I think some justification for the view taken of it by Mr Goddard. So far as it lays down that under the Statute when a right has been made indefeasible no difference has been made, it is clearly in the teeth of *Tapling v. Jones*, and therefore of no value. It includes too much. But so far as what is included in the larger proposition goes, viz. that although until a right becomes indefeasible under the Act no difference is made except the fixing of a definite period of enjoyment, and that even where the right has become indefeasible under the Statute as well as before that time it can be also claimed at Common Law as before the Act, I think he is clearly right. That this is the proper view seems plain from the subsequent case of *Aynsley v. Glover*, 10 Ch. 285. Mellish, L. J., in the course of the argument, says, " It is every day practice to plead (1) enjoyment for 20 years before action; (2) enjoyment for 40 years before action; (3) enjoyment from time immemorial; (4) lost grant; and it has always been understood that a right may be supported on the third ground although it may be incapable of being supported under the first or second. There are no negative words in the Statute to take away rights existing independently of it." And again in the judgment in which James, L. J., concurred, he says, " The Statute 2 and 3 Will. IV. c. 71 has not, as I apprehend, taken away any of the modes of claiming easements which existed before that Statute. Indeed as the Statute requires the twenty years or forty years (as the case may be), the enjoyment during which confers a right, to be the twenty years or forty years next immediately before some suit or action is brought with respect to the easement, there would be a variety of valuable easements which would be altogether destroyed if a Plaintiff was not entitled to resort to the proof which he could have resorted to before the Act passed." It is, I submit, quite clear from this that *Tapling v. Jones* did not lay down any such proposition as is contended for by Mr Goddard. To sum up then, the result appears to be that until the period of indefeasibility is reached the only effect of the Act is to shorten or define the period required for prescription: after the period of indefeasibility is reached, the Act makes a statutory grant of the right without regard to the Common Law: except that as regards cases coming under Sections 1 and 2, though not in cases of light, the claim must be to a right that could have been claimed by custom, prescription or grant. As to this see *Earl de la Warr v. Miles*, 17 Ch. D. 535, where at p. 591 Brett, L. J., says, "When those two things (the enjoyment for 60 or 40 years, as of right) have been proved the question whether the Statute is applicable depends upon a pure question of law—are those acts which have been done, such that a right to do them could arise by custom or prescription or grant— not whether a right to do them was claimed as a matter of prescription or custom or grant, but whether a right to do them could have been the subject-matter of a prescription or custom or grant?"

And then either before or after the period is reached the right may be claimed alternatively at Common Law. There are several further matters in the first section that require comment. They are however common to the second and third sections also. I therefore omit them until after dealing with the matters peculiar to those sections.

The second section provides :—

"And be it further enacted that no claim which may be lawfully made at the common law by custom prescription or grant to any way or other easement or to any watercourse or the use of any water to be enjoyed or derived upon over or from any land or water of our said Lord the King his heirs or successors or being parcel of the Duchy of Lancaster or of the Duchy of Cornwall or being the property of an ecclesiastical or lay person or body corporate when such way or other matter as herein last before mentioned shall have been actually enjoyed by any person claiming right thereto without interruption for the full period of twenty years shall be defeated or destroyed by showing only that such way or other matter was first enjoyed at any time prior to such period of twenty years but nevertheless such claim may be defeated in any other way by which the same is now liable to be defeated and where such way or other matter as herein last before mentioned shall have been so enjoyed as aforesaid for the full period of forty years the right thereto shall be deemed absolute and indefeasible unless it shall appear that the same was enjoyed by some consent or agreement expressly given or made for that purpose by deed or writing."

The most important point that has come for decision upon the construction of this section is, What is the meaning of the word easement there used ? Does it mean any easement whatever, or only easements ejusdem generis with ways, or what else ?

In the first place I think it is plain that it does not mean any easement whatever, but only easements as limited and defined by the further provisions of the section, as will presently appear. That appears from *Webb v. Bird*, 13 C. B. N. S. 841, where Erle, C. J., in his judgment not only thought that it did not apply to every easement, but expressed his opinion that it applied only to the two classes of easements mentioned, viz. ways or watercourses.

In the same case Byles, J., thought the section only applied to easements ejusdem generis with a way. But he in the same breath said that in so doing he was agreeing with the judgment of Erle, C. J.

Now it will be observed that the right, whatever it is, must have been enjoyed *without interruption* for the required period. It has therefore been held, and upon this point there is, I think, no discrepancy of opinion, that the right must in any event be such an one as is capable of being interrupted (see *Webb v. Bird*, sup., and judgment of Lord Selborne in *Angus v. Dalton*, 6 App. Cas. 740), and that by means that are reasonable, *Arkwright v. Gell*, 5 M. and W. 203. It is said (Goddard, p. 183) that the authorities, so far as they have construed this word in the second section of the Act, are in direct conflict. But I think that, although the point is still, for want of further decision, left in some obscurity, if the authorities in

question are carefully examined, there is no sufficient reason
for considering them to be in conflict. Now upon the point
that the right must be one capable of being interrupted, all
the judges in *Webb v. Bird*, 10 C. B. N. S. 841, Lord Abinger
in *Arkwright v. Gell*, 5 M. and W. 264, and Lord Selborne and
Coleridge in *Angus v. Dalton*, 6 App. Cas., are in accord. As
to that Erle, C. J., is clearly of opinion that it is so (at p. 283),
and although he does say (p. 282) that it appears to him that
the section applies only to ways and watercourses, he does
not give that as a confident opinion. In the same case
Willes, J., at p. 285, apparently, though it is not quite clear,
thinks that a claim to support, the right in question in *Angus
v. Dalton*, was within the meaning of the second section. It
would therefore follow that although he concurred in the
judgment of Erle, C. J., he would still have been prepared
to decide *Angus v. Dalton* in the same way, and for the same
reasons as Lord Selborne. And then Byles, J., in his judgment
(at p. 286), says he agrees with Erle, C. J., that it must be
ejusdem generis with a way, in the sense that it is to be
exercised upon or over the soil of the adjoining owner. For my
part, I find it not quite easy to see how, if that be the ground
of exclusion, this right to the access of air came to be excluded.
It clearly is enjoyed over the adjoining land. It seems therefore
decidedly preferable to exclude it for the reason stated by
Willes, J., that the right was too inconvenient and impracticable
to be recognised, or as Lord Selborne puts it, "the point then
determined (as I understand it) was that a claim to have
free access for all the winds of heaven to the sails of a windmill
was too large and indefinite in its nature to be acquired by
use." Now it will be apparent that if all that was decided in
Webb v. Bird was that the right must be capable of interruption, and that the right to access of air was too indefinite
to be included, and that, be it observed, not so much on the
ground whether it was ejusdem generis with ways, as on the
ground that it was not even a right that could have been
claimed at Common Law (see judgment of Willes, J.), then
there is no discrepancy of opinion whatsoever. This, after a
careful reading of the authorities, I certainly take to be the

effect of the case, and I am therefore again unable to agree
with Mr Goddard. But if it be objected that the opinions of
the judges in *Webb v. Bird* must be taken, that the right must
be ejusdem generis with ways, then comes the question, in the
absence of any indication from the judges, how many points of
similarity did they severally require to constitute a right of the
same genus with a way? Are we to take the dictum of
Erle, C. J., to mean that they must be identical to be ejusdem
generis? Is the capability of interruption a sufficient common
characteristic? In this case it will be observed that Lord
Selborne would be in agreement with them. Or must the
definition of Byles, J., be accepted that in order to be ejusdem
generis with a way the right must not only be capable of interruption, but must also be exercised upon or over the soil of the
adjoining owner, and that interpreted by the fact that he
held a right to access of air not exercised over the adjoining
land? If this last definition be adopted it would appear
still to make the decisions reconcilable. It would leave it to
be a question in each case whether the particular right claimed
was of the required nature, and we should be left merely with
Webb v. Bird, a decision that access of air was not such a right,
and *Angus v. Dalton*, a decision that a right of support is such
a right: two perfectly consistent decisions. See further *Bryant
v. Lefever*, 4 C. P. D. 172, *Sturges v. Bridgman*, 11 Ch. D.
355.

There appears to me therefore no great difficulty in distinguishing the other cases where the same question has been
debated. *Mounsey v. Ismay*, 3 H. and C. 486, is quoted as a
difficulty. But the saying of Cotton, L. J., that a case is worth
nothing until it is thoroughly examined, is nowhere more true
than in cases upon the Prescription Act; and if that solvent be
applied to *Mounsey v. Ismay* any apparent inconsistency will be
dissipated. It was there decided that a custom to hold races
upon a certain piece of land was not an easement at all. That
being so there was no ground for saying that it came within
the second section. No question could arise. This decision is
obviously right. There can be no such thing as an easement
in gross (see Williams on *Commons*); an easement requires a

dominant and servient tenement (see Goddard, p. 2, definition). And although it is said in *Mounsey v. Ismay*, p. 498, "we are not prepared to say that the statute may not extend to easements in gross" on the ground that Lord Wensleydale in *Welcome v. Upton*, 6 M. and W. 536, had expressed some inclination to hold that the right there in question, which is said to be an easement in gross, was within the equity of the Statute; yet when *Welcome v. Upton* is examined the right there in question is found not to be an easement of any kind, but a profit a prendre which no one has ever suggested to be incapable of existing in gross.

There are several other cases mentioned by Mr Goddard, see *Bliss v. Hall*, 4 Bing. N. C. 183, *Flight v. Thomas*, 10 A. and E. 590: but they really add nothing of value upon this point as they were decided upon subsidiary questions.[1]

It has been held also upon the construction of the word easement in the second section, that it must be an easement pure and simple with no ulterior view of profit. That the second section cannot be used to substantiate claims to profits though they be claimed merely in the guise of an easement, when the only object of the user of the easement would be to obtain a profit.

Thus in *Bailey v. Appleyard*, 8 A. and E. 161, it was held that an easement to turn cattle into a lane could not be claimed under the second section, when the only object of so turning them out was to obtain the profit of pasturage.

The word watercourse has acquired several meanings, the primary and proper meaning being I take it the flow of water; it is intended to be a translation of aquæ cursus. Watercourses therefore should be rights in connexion with flowing streams (see Coulson and Forbes on *Waters*, p. 51). It has however acquired other meanings, *e.g.* the bed, and the stream. See Goddard, p. 187.

Jessel, M. R., in *Taylor v. Corporation of St Helens*, 6 Ch. D. 264, says, "A grant of a watercourse in Law, especially when coupled with other words, may mean certainly one of two things, if not one of three things. It may mean the easement or the right to the running water; it may mean the channel pipe or drain which contains the water: and it may mean the

---

[1] At any rate it is clear that the 2nd section does not include light. *Percy v. Eames*, 1891, 1 Ch. 658.

land over which the water flows.......*I do not see how water-course standing alone can mean anything but the flow of the water.*" Now in the Prescription Act the word is used in its proper sense as rights in connexion with the flow of water. It certainly does not mean rights to the mere use of water, for that is separately provided for, and there is no ground for saying that it means either the channel in which the water flows, or the land over which the water flows. But apparently under the Act the word must be construed in the wide sense of any rights in connexion with the flow of water. Thus it includes a right to pollute a running stream, *Carlyon v. Lovering*, 1 H. and N. 784; or a right to have a stream diverted, *Mason v. Shrewsbury and Hereford Ry. Co.*, L. R. 6 Q. B. 578; or a right to send water flowing over the land of another, *Wright v. Williams*, 1 M. and W. 77. And although a water-course according to Angell (*Watercourses*, 30) consists of (1) the bed, (2) the bank or shore, (3) the water; yet it is quite clear that under the Act the word can only mean the right to the flow of the water, and that the ownership of the land is immaterial. Otherwise no right to the water could be established by prescription since there can be no prescription for land. And it is quite clear on the very best authority that so long as a person has a right of access to the water by owning land on the bank, that is so long as he is a riparian owner, the ownership of the bed of the stream is unimportant. As to this there is ample authority.

 Lyon v. Fishmongers' Co. 1 App. Cas. 662.

 Chasemore v. Richards, 7 H. L. 382.

 Embrey v. Owen, 6 Ex. 369.

Following upon this the right to the "use of water" must probably be restricted to rights in connexion with water not as a running stream.

The third section provides:—

"And be it further enacted that when the access and use of light to and for any dwelling-house workshop or other building shall have been actually enjoyed therewith for the full period of twenty years without interruption the right thereto shall be deemed absolute and indefeasible any local usage or custom to the contrary notwithstanding unless it shall appear that the same was enjoyed by some consent or agreement expressly made or given for that purpose by deed or writing."

Now the first thing to notice is that the use of light is not required to be that of any window, it is the use of light for any dwelling-house, workshop or other building.

The nature of the right to light has recently, *Scott v. Pape,* 31 Ch. D. 554, been put upon a definite and intelligible footing. It was then decided that the right was a right to the cone of light that was wont to come over the servient tenement, and be enjoyed by the dominant tenement. So that the right is not in the least affected by the mere fact that the apertures through which it was enjoyed are advanced or set back, so long as they catch in their new position substantially the same cone of light. But of course the light cannot be increased by advancing them though it may be partially lost by setting them back.

The provision as to local usage or custom here has the effect of abolishing an old custom of London, that so long as a new house was built on the same foundations as an old one, it might be raised though it blocked up ancient lights, *Hughes v. Kerne,* Yelv. 215, *Truscott v. Merchant Taylors' Co.,* 11 Ex. 855. It is to be observed that the light must be enjoyed in connexion with a building : a piece of ground unbuilt upon acquires no right to light. This provision is merely in accord with a previous decision, see *Roberts v. Macord,* 1 Moo. and Rob. 230 ; and *Potts v. Smith,* 6 Eq. 311. But there is no necessity that people with eyes to enjoy the light should actually inhabit the building: the mere structure alone is sufficient to acquire the right. *Courtauld v. Legh,* L. R., 4 Ex. 126.

The claim to light under the Act differs from that to other rights[1] in that the 3rd section does not require the claim to be one that could have been made by custom, prescription or grant, and there is no necessity that the enjoyment should have been as of right. This makes the right to light conferred by the Statute, a right of an entirely new kind.

Further, it must be observed that there is no preliminary period with regard to light, but when once the twenty years have elapsed the right is indefeasible. I said twenty years, but

H.   [1] So no right to light can be acquired against the Crown.   3
Percy v. Eames, 1891, 1 Ch. 658.

I must now show that it is not quite twenty years that is required.

The construction of these words came in question in *Flight v. Thomas*, 11 A. and E. 688, 8 Cl. and F. 231. That was a case of a most peculiar nature. There light had been enjoyed for nineteen years and the beginning of a twentieth. During the twentieth year the right was interrupted; but at the expiration of the twentieth year, and before the interruption had continued for a year an action was brought against the person so interrupting. The section provides that the right must be actually enjoyed for the full period of twenty years without interruption. Nothing could appear more plain. But section 4 provides that " No Act or other matter shall be deemed to be an interruption within the meaning of this Statute unless the same shall have been or shall be submitted to or acquiesced in for one year after the party interrupted shall have had or shall have notice thereof." It was clear therefore that at the end of the twentieth year the right had been enjoyed ' without interruption ' within the meaning of the Act, and the only question was whether it had been actually enjoyed, and it was held that it had. See too *Glover v. Coleman*, L. R., 10 C. P. 108, where the interruption had not in fact been acquiesced in. It follows therefore that the period required is not twenty years, but in any event only a little over nineteen, and it may be less when the interruption is found as a fact not to have been acquiesced in. But of course though, as soon as nineteen years and a day have passed the right is one that will eventually hold good, no action can be brought until a year after, when the twenty years have elapsed.

The first of the requirements common to the three first sections is that of actual enjoyment. There has been some discussion as to the meaning of this according to the terms of the Act, and the decisions have been undoubtedly conflicting. The chief difficulty has arisen in the case of rights, the enjoyment of which is intermittent in such a way that the user only takes place perhaps at intervals of two or three years.

Of course when a right is of a continuous nature there is not the same difficulty : it either has or has not been enjoyed for the required period; and evidence that it was being enjoyed before the beginning of the period required by the Act and that it is being enjoyed at the present time would in the absence of proof of non-enjoyment or interruption, be sufficient to show actual enjoyment under the Act.

But with regard to rights of that intermittent nature that are only required to be exercised by their owners at intervals of years the law had been reduced by conflicting decisions to a state of the utmost uncertainty and the most hopeless confusion, from which it has at length been rescued by a luminous and masterly judgment of the Court of Appeal. I must first show how the confusion arose and then expound the cure.

In the first place there was some sort of authority for saying that the Prescription Act did not apply at all to rights which were not exercised at least once every year. There is a dictum of Parke, B., to that effect in *Lowe v. Carpenter*, 6 Ex. 25, adopted and enlarged by Coleridge, C. J., in *Hollins v. Verney*, 11 Q. B. D. 715.

He there says, "It does not appear to me to be an easement capable of being claimed under the Prescription Act. In the words of Parke, B., it seems to be one of those cases in which the Statute cannot be taken to apply 'where the rights mentioned in it are used at intervals of two or three years, for in such cases a party could not acquiesce for one year under the 4th section of the Act if the act or matter is done only at intervals of two or three years.'"

This difficulty was noticed by Lindley, L. J., in the Court of Appeal in *Hollins v. Verney*, 13 Q. B. D. 309, and though the Court did not assent to the principle yet as a difficulty it was not answered in that clean and satisfactory manner desirable in interpreting an Act of Parliament. The way it is left now is this, "The truth is that the question whether in any particular case a right of way has, or has not" (the right in question was a right of way, but the words of course apply equally to any analogous right) "been actually enjoyed for the full period of twenty years, appears to be left by the Act to be treated as a question of fact to be decided by a jury, unless the Court sees that having regard to section 6 and the other provisions of the

Statute there is no evidence on which the jury can properly find such enjoyment." It seems to me that this difficulty arises through not clearly apprehending what is an interruption within the meaning of the Act. It is quite true that the only rights within the Act are rights capable of being interrupted: that is capable of being put an end to by an interruption as defined by the Act. Now according to section 4, nothing is to be deemed an interruption unless it is acquiesced in for a year. Therefore it is said that rights only exercised once in two or three years are not capable of interruption. It is difficult to see how this follows when the true nature of an interruption under the Act is considered. An interruption is not an intermission (see judgment of Denman, C. J., in *Carr v. Foster*, 3 Q. B. 586); according to Patteson, J., in the same case "Interruption in section 1 must clearly mean an obstruction by the act of some other person than the claimant." And William, J., "Interruption means an obstruction. There must be an overt act indicating that the right is disputed."

If therefore there be that overt act, and it be acquiesced in for a year that is an interruption, albeit there were no desire to exercise the right during the year. But the real difficulty and absurdity from which the law has now been rescued was this. The authority was practically unanimous that in order to establish a claim under the Act to a right of an intermittent nature it was necessary to give direct evidence of actual user during the last year of the period. That was decided in *Parker v. Mitchell*, 11 A. and E. 790. See *Lowe v. Carpenter*, 6 Ex. at p. 832, and *Hollins v. Verney*, 11 Q. B. D. at p. 718. Then there was authority which was apparently regarded as satisfactory, that there must be the same direct evidence of user during the first year.

The first case was *Bailey v. Appleyard*, 8 A. and E. 161: but that case does not seem to decide that a right naturally only used at intervals of several years must have been put in exercise in the first year of the prescriptive period where there has been no interruption, and where there has been user prior to that year. However there cannot be any doubt that it has been taken by the Courts to have decided that.

See *Lowe v. Carpenter, ubi sup., Hollins v. Verney,* 11 Q. B. D. 710.

But it is quite clear that no direct evidence of user during each of the intervening years was ever required. All that need be found by the jury is that the right has been substantially in a real and positive manner, having regard to its nature, enjoyed during each and every year of the prescriptive period. This is the clear decision of the case of *Carr v. Foster,* 3 Q. B. 584.

This case was noticed in *Lowe v. Carpenter,* and the judges then, though they thought there must be direct evidence given in the first and the last year, yet were quite prepared to hold that that was not necessary during the intervening years. Alderson, B., there after noticing *Parker v. Mitchell* and *Bailey v. Appleyard,* says " *Carr v. Foster* seems to intimate that the intermediate time is not so material. Whether that distinction be sound or not, it appears to me to be a very convenient one: for one or two witnesses might be sufficient to prove the enjoyment at the commencement and expiration of the time, whereas it might require forty witnesses to prove the exercise of the enjoyment during the whole of the intermediate time."

That then was the state of the law. Surely nothing could be more unsatisfactory. That condition has now been entirely changed and the law has been freed from technicality so far as possible in the case of an Act of the technical nature of the Prescription Act, and has been placed again upon a basis of sound common sense. That was by the decision of the Court of Appeal in *Hollins v. Verney,* 13 Q. B. D. 304.

The effect of that decision is this. The question is in every case for the jury. They are to say whether there has been an actual substantial enjoyment having regard to the nature of the right by the person claiming it whenever he wished to do so. No direct evidence of user in the first, the last, or any of the intervening years is required and evidence of user before the period is admissible. At the same time it may be that in any particular case the Court may as a question of law upon the construction of the Act hold that the right claimed does not come within it. And the Court held that in that particular case the right, which was a right of way exercised in the year before action, again twelve years before that, and again twelve years before that, was of too discontinuous a nature to be within the Act. The particular ground for so holding appears at p. 315, "It is sufficient for the present case to observe that the Statute expressly requires actual enjoyment as of right for the period of twenty years before action. No user can be sufficient which does not raise a reasonable inference of such a continuous enjoyment. Moreover, as the enjoyment which is pointed out by the Statute is an enjoyment which is open as well as of right, it seems to follow that no actual user can be sufficient to satisfy the Statute, unless during the whole of the statutory term (whether acts of user be proved in each year or not) the user is enough at any rate to carry to the mind of a reasonable person who is in possession of the servient tenement, the fact that a continuous right to enjoyment is being asserted, and ought to be resisted if such right is not recognised, and if resistance to it is intended. Can an user which is confined to the rare occasions on which the alleged right is supposed in this instance to have been exercised, satisfy even this test? It seems to us that it cannot: that it is not and could not reasonably be treated as the assertion of a continuous right to enjoy; and when there is no assertion by conduct of a continuous right to enjoy, it appears to us that there cannot be an actual enjoyment within the meaning of the Statute. Without therefore professing to be able to draw the line sharply between long and short periods of non-user, without holding that non-user for a year or even more is necessarily fatal in all cases, without attempting to define that which the Statute has left indefinite we are of opinion that no jury can properly find that the right claimed by the defendant in this case has been established by evidence of such limited user as was mainly relied upon."

And again at p. 314, "We confess however that we do not appreciate the supposed distinction between a temporary non-user for a year occurring at the beginning or the end or in the middle of the statutory period. *Flight v. Thomas* and the language of section 4 show that an interruption for a year is fatal, and that an interruption for less than a year is not fatal, whether it occurs at the commencement, or end, or at any part of the statutory period, so a cessation given which excludes an inference of actual enjoyment as of right for the full statutory period will be fatal at whatsoever portion of the period the cessation occurs ; and on the other hand a cessation given which does not exclude such inference is not fatal, even although it occurs at the end of the period there can be no subsequent user to explain it, and the inference of actual enjoyment for the full period next before action is more difficult to draw than in other cases. But we are not prepared to say that as a matter of law such an inference can in no case be drawn."

It will appear therefore to be clear that generally under the Act, subject only to what has already been said, the question of actual enjoyment is a question for the jury.

The right is required to have been actually enjoyed *for the full period specified* by the Act. Hence of course if there has been an intermission by the voluntary act of the claimant, the time can only begin to count from the resumption of the enjoyment after the intermission. The enjoyment must be a continuous enjoyment. Of course when the right is not of a continuous nature, common sense, as Lindley, L. J., says in *Hollins v. Verney*, explains that it is not required to be put in use every minute. But the user must be such that, having regard to the nature of the right in question, it cannot be said that the owner has not used it at any time when he might reasonably have required to do. See judgment of Brett, L. J., in *Earl De la Warr v. Miles*, 17 Ch. D. p. 591. And where there has been an enjoyment with several intermissions the time will only begin to count from the termination of the last ; although if the various periods of enjoyment were taken and added together they might collectively amount to the required length of time. This is clearly laid down by Parke, B., in *Onley v. Gardiner*, 4 M. and W. 500. " We are all clearly of opinion that in order to entitle the defendant to the benefit of the statutory plea it must be an enjoyment of the easement as such and as of right for a continuous period of twenty years next before the suit without such interruption as is defined on the Act, upon which nothing turns in this case...to hold that the words might be satisfied by an enjoyment for different intervals, which added together would be twenty years, the last continuing up to the commencement of the suit, would be to let in a great number of cases in which the presumption of a grant never could have existed before the Statute. For instance if the occupier had used the road openly for a year or two and then uniformly asked permission on each occasion, or only used it secretly and by stealth, for some years, and then resumed the enjoyment of it, no one would contend that a grant could have been presumed because the intervals of enjoyment united might amount to twenty years."

The same seems to follow from the decision in *Monmouth Canal Co. v. Harford*, 1 C. M. and R. p. 64. Lord Lyndhurst there (p. 631) says, "The simple issue is whether there has been a continued enjoyment of the way for twenty years, and any evidence negativing the continuance is admissible."

In the same way when there has been unity of possession of the dominant and servient tenements no easement can have been actually enjoyed within the meaning of the Act, unless it has been so enjoyed for twenty years after the severance. This appears in the judgment in *Bright v. Walker*, 1 C. M. and R. at p. 219, "In the same way no title would be acquired if there had been unity of possession during all or part of the time, for then the claimant would not have enjoyed as of right the easement but the soil itself."

So in *Onley v. Gardiner, sup.*, Parke, B., says,

"A similar reason applies to intervals of unity of possession during which there is no one who could complain of the user of the road. It would be no answer to say that in one particular case, where the land over which the right is exercised is out on lease, the legislature had provided for the non-continuity, if I may so say, of one of the periods mentioned in the Act. But in truth it has not so provided for the effect of the 8th section is not to unite discontinuous periods of enjoyment, but to extend the period of continuous enjoyment, which is necessary to give a right by so long a time as the land is out on lease, subject to the condition therein mentioned. It appears to us therefore that according to the words and meaning of the Act the enjoyment of the easement must be continuous, and the Court has already intimated its opinion to that effect in *Monmouth Canal Co. v. Harford*, That an enjoyment must be of an easement *as such* is a matter on which we feel no difficulty."

See *Harbidge v. Warwick*, 3 Ex. 552; *Battishill v. Reed*, 18 C. B. 696.

There is a dictum of Lord Hatherley to the contrary effect in *Ladyman v. Grove*, 6 Ch. p. 768; but it was not necessary to the decision, and appears also to be founded upon some confusion between user that is interrupted within the meaning of the Act, and user that is found not to have actually taken place. He says, "Undoubtedly, as in the case of all other easements, the accruing right to the easement is suspended, but suspended only during the union of the possession, so that if it had been shown that the enjoyment had lasted for fifteen years and upwards, and then had been interrupted by unity of possession, and then the enjoyment had lasted for five years more without the unity of possession, in such a case an enjoyment for twenty years could have been pleaded. The interruption, if such it may be called, by the unity of possession is not an interruption in the sense indicated by the Statute, which means an adverse interruption."

This would of course apply also to an intermission arising by the voluntary act of the claimant unconnected with unity of possession. It is however an isolated dictum without consideration of the cases to the contrary, and is, it is submitted, wrong in law.

Another requirement of the Act is that the enjoyment should have been by a person claiming right thereto, §§ 1, 2, or as it may be pleaded, § 5, claiming "as a right," except that in the case of light under § 3, the claim of right is not required.

Now it is by no means easy to gather from the cases when a claim can be said to have been as of right within the meaning of the Statute. One or two points however are plain. In order that the claim may be as of right, the enjoyment must have been in the language of the Civil Law, nec vi nec clam nec precario[1]. It must not have been vi; not merely not enjoyed by force of arms, but not enjoyed under show of resistance, that is, it must have been peaceable. I do not think that the objection made by Mr Goddard (p. 230) to such an enjoyment that "it is impossible that any presumption of a grant can arise from that kind of user" is a valid one. Because the title gained under the Act is not founded on any presumption of a grant as at Common Law, but is absolutely conferred by the Act, the only thing is that as the Act was intended to establish no rights other than rights of such a nature that they could have been in proper circumstances gained at Common Law, it requires the rights to be of such a nature that they could have been granted. And it may well be that a right similar to the one in dispute might have been granted. Again the exercise of a right may be as of right though another party may out of mistake or malice dispute it. Now every right under the Act must be enjoyed as against some servient owner. If he does some act showing an intention to dispute the right and that is acquiesced in for a year, the right has not been enjoyed without interruption. But supposing the claimant does not acquiesce but the right is continually disputed, can it be said to be enjoyed at all? Laws are made for the purpose of restraining violence: the Act contemplates and was passed to regulate the acquisition of rights under the ordinary peaceful course of everyday life, and does not apply to a case of a claim which a man cannot assert "without danger of being treated as a trespasser." See *Tickle v. Brown*, 4 A. and E. 369.

When the exercise of the right has only been during a perpetual contention, though it may be claimed as of right, yet the enjoyment is not as of right, i.e. as if the claim were a rightful one. As Lord Campbell says in *Eaton v. Swansea W. W. Co.*, 17 Q. B. 274:

"Interruptions acquiesced in for less than a year may be of great weight as evidence on the question whether there ever was a commencement of an enjoyment as of right. Such inter-

---

[1] Dig. lib. 39, tit. 3, de aqua, § 23 ; *Eaton v. Swansea W. W. Co.*, 17 Q. B. 275.

ruptions are explanatory of what the user really was. I think it would be a monstrous state of law if this were not so."

The enjoyment must not be clam; it must be open. This follows from the requirement that it shall be peaceable. If the claimant had not concealed his enjoyment, it might have been disputed. And in any event concealed enjoyment is not one that on the face of it looks like a rightful one. So much is plain. But then the enjoyment must not be precario: it must not be enjoyed by permission.

This is a more difficult question. This much seems clear that the enjoyment is not as of right if permission is asked occasionally within the prescriptive period. As is said by Parke, B., in *Bright v. Walker*, 1 C. M. and R. at p. 219 :

" Therefore if the way shall appear to have been enjoyed by the claimant not openly and in the manner that a person rightfully entitled would have used it, but by stealth as a trespasser would have done—if he shall have occasionally asked the permission of the occupier of the land—no title would be acquired because it was not enjoyed as of right." And again, Denman, C. J., in *Tickle v. Brown*, 4 A. and E. at p. 382, says " It seems therefore that the enjoyment as of right must mean an enjoyment had not secretly or by stealth or by tacit sufferance, or by permission asked from time to time on each occasion, or even on many occasions, of using it ; but an enjoyment had openly, notoriously, without particular leave at the time by a person claiming to use it without danger of being treated as a trespasser as a matter of right, whether strictly legal by prescription and adverse user or by deed conferring the right, or though not strictly legal, yet lawful to the extent of excusing a trespass, as by consent or agreement in writing not under seal in case of a plea for forty years, or by such writing or parole consent or agreement contract or license in case of a plea for twenty years."

And the reason of this is given by Lord Lyndhurst in *Monmouth Canal Company v. Harford*, 1 C. M. and R. p. 631 :

" Every time that the occupiers asked for leave they admitted that the former licence had expired and that the continuance of the enjoyment was broken." It seems to me however that the words of Lord Denman in *Tickle v. Brown* are consistent with a state of law other than it appears to be. So far as I can ascertain it, it is this. When the period of indefeasibility has been reached the right is not defeated by showing any agreement prior to the period except a deed or agreement in writing; but it would be defeated by showing that permission had been *verbally given within the period,* since the enjoyment would then not have been as of right. With regard to the primary prescriptive period the right is defeated by showing permission granted verbally, and a fortiori by deed or writing within the period (*Tone v. Preston,* 24 Ch. D. 739) and apparently by deed or writing before the period and extending over the whole period. For it would be absurd if the right were to be so defeated when enjoyed for the period of indefeasibility, but not when only enjoyed for the primary period. It seems however that a verbal permission given before and extending over the whole, or given before and extending over part, the right being exercised continually for the rest of the primary period, does not defeat but is consistent with an enjoyment as of right. This appears from the judgment of Alderson, B., in *Kinlock v. Nevile,* 6 M. and W. p. 806, "If a parole permission extends over the whole of the twenty years the party enjoys the way as of right and without interruption for the twenty years: not so if the leave given be from time to time within the twenty years."

But a permission given by deed or writing before and extending over part, the enjoyment being continued during the rest of the primary period, may defeat the right. This appears from the actual decision in *Kinlock v. Nevile, sup.* That was an action of trespass: plea a right of way: replication set forth an Act of Parliament under which prior to the twenty years a towing-path, over which the right of way was claimed, had been made. It then went on to show that after the commencement of the period by another Act another towing-path was substituted. The defendant had prior to the period used the path under the Act, but when, upon the substitution of the new path, his rights under the Act had terminated, he still continued to use the old path without interruption until action brought. It

was held that the replication was good ; for although his enjoyment was of right and without interruption, yet the Act of
Parliament was a deed or writing which showed that he only
had it for a limited period. It is to be observed that had the
permission not been in writing the result would have been
different. It would have been held then that the right being
of a kind that could be granted a verbal agreement could not
after the expiration of the twenty years be put in evidence to
show that it had not in fact been granted for ever. As it was,
although the right was of a kind that could be granted, yet the
agreement being of the prescribed kind could be produced to
show that it had not in fact been granted for good. This is
quite in accordance with the policy of the Act the object of
which was to quiet disputes where length of time was likely to
render the evidence unsatisfactory[1].

The way this is arrived at is by a consideration of the
sections of the Act as is done by Lord Denman in *Tickle v.
Brown, sup.* He there says, " As all these matters " (*i.e.* those
mentioned in § 5) "are required to be specially pleaded and
forbidden to be given in evidence under a general traverse of
the enjoyment as of right, it is plain that they are treated by
the legislature as consistent with such enjoyment; and as by
the rules of pleading and of logical reasoning every allegation
by way of answer which does not deny the matter to which it
is proposed as an answer, is taken to confess it, we must conclude that the legislature used the words ' as of right ' in such
a sense as that a party confessing the enjoyment ' as of right '
for forty years or twenty as the case may be, may account for
and avoid the effect of it by alleging, in the one case, a consent
or agreement, provided if it be by deed or writing (see § 2) and
in the other any contract &c., written or parole (see § 5), it
follows that the words ' as of right ' cannot be confined to an
adverse right from all time as far as evidence shows, for if they
were so confined, such enjoyment once confessed could not be
avoided by replying that it was held by contract which is not
adverse. Again, as the legal right to a way cannot pass except

---

[1] See 1st Rep. of R. P. Commissioners, introduction to Prescription and
Limitation.

by deed it is plain that the words 'enjoyment as of right' cannot be confined to enjoyment under a strict legal right, for then a consent or agreement in writing *not under seal* of which the 2nd section speaks could not account for such enjoyment. The words therefore must have a wider sense."

It would seem therefore that with regard to claims under §§ 1 and 2 if the right was enjoyed by a parole agreement made before the commencement of the period, under which the claimant was to pay a rent, and he did so pay it for the whole of the period, he could at the end of the period cease paying the rent, and establish his right under the Act.

And it is clear that this would be so in case of claim to light under the 3rd section, for the enjoyment there is not required to be as of right.

And just as the actual enjoyment is required to be a continuous enjoyment for the full period, so must the enjoyment "as of right" have been continuous: so that just in the same way as a break in the continuity of the actual enjoyment is fatal, so also is an intermission in the enjoyment as of right.

Another requirement of the enjoyment common to these three sections, is that it shall be without interruption. The 4th section defines what an interruption is. It provides that nothing is to be deemed an interruption unless acquiesced in for a year. And the judicial interpretation of the section has already been given in the judgments in *Carr v. Foster*. The peculiar effect of the 4th section upon the period of prescription with regard to light was settled in *Flight v. Thomas* and that of course applies to other rights within the Prescription Act.

It will be observed that the first provision of the 4th section deals with the time from which the prescriptive periods are to be reckoned. The section runs as follows:—

" And be it further enacted that each of the respective periods of years hereinbefore mentioned shall be deemed and taken to be the period next before some suit or action, wherein the claim or matter to which such period may relate shall have been or shall be brought into question."

The plain reading of this would certainly, I think, lead one to the conclusion, which has ultimately been adopted by the

Courts, viz.: that when once there has been an action in which the right in question was the subject of judicial determination, that then in any subsequent action disputing it there is no necessity to show user for the period next before such second action. The right so established in the first action then became indefeasible. But it was argued in *Cooper v. Hubbuck*, 12 C. B. pp. 54, 56, that the effect of the section was that in every action with regard to the right the user for the period immediately preceding must be shown. That might have been a possible reading of the words of the section if "any suit or action" were substituted for "some suit or action"; and in some cases the judges appear to have so read it. But even then the construction desired could hardly have been adopted, since in that case no right would ever become indefeasible under the Act: a result contrary not only to the whole purpose of the Statute, passed as it was to quiet titles, but also to the express words providing for indefeasibility of title.

The argument of Williams, J., who differed from the majority of the Court in *Cooper v. Hubbuck* was that the other construction had already been adopted by the Court in the judgment in *Wright v. Williams*, 1 M. and W. 77, when Lord Abinger had said with regard to the agreement that no right could be established under the Act unless some action were brought "to which it may be added that one action could not perfect the title to the right as the Act requires an enjoyment for the full period immediately before *any* action." It will be seen that not only does Lord Abinger misread the words of the section, substituting "any" for "some," but his opinion is a mere dictum, and was certainly not considered as binding authority, for in the subsequent case of *Richards v. Fry*, 7 A. and E. 698, Lord Denman certainly considers the point as open, for he says, "We hold that the only correct averment is next before the commencement of this (or possibly some other) suit." And his chief further argument was that the legislature could never have intended the result which would follow if that construction were adopted, viz. that if the right had been enjoyed for the required period next before some action, which however never went to trial but was dropped, that then it should be established. The practical answer to that has certainly justified itself. No such case has ever come into the Courts and if it did, it may well be that an action which is dropped would be held to be not an action within the meaning of the Act. However as no case has arisen within sixty years, the anomaly, if such it be, does not seem to be of any pressing moment. Certainly the argument ab inconvenienti is all the other way. One point is well put by Willes, J., at p. 469, "There is no estoppel, no plea of res judicata as to the right upon a plea or subsequent pleading under Lord Tenterden's Act, unless enjoyment before a former suit or action may be pleaded as in the present case. And here what an anomaly would result! In all cases in which the right might have been alleged generally before the Act, it may by the 5th section be now so alleged: and a finding upon a traverse of the right would be conclusive in a subsequent action. So that, if the dominant owner brings an action alleging in his declaration his right generally, and a disturbance of it, and upon a traverse of the right the plaintiff makes out his case under the Act and has a verdict, that verdict is conclusive in a subsequent action. But if the owner of the servient tenement bring an action and the dominant owner under the same section plead an enjoyment for the period mentioned in the Statute ending with the commencement of the action, and that is traversed and found for him, according to the defendant's argument it only decides the particular suit, and is of no avail except perhaps as merely evidence in a subsequent action which seems a strange and inconsistent result." He very wisely held that the words "shall have been" was not to be restricted to actions pending at the passing of the Act, as had been argued. And generally upon the broad ground the majority of the Court was of opinion that the intention of the Act was to confer a right good for all time, not merely to settle the dispute for purposes of the one action in question. With regard to the question of interruption there has been a recent decision of interest from the point of view of practice. It has been decided that in an action for obstruction of light, and presumably the same principle would apply to all interruptions under the Act, if it appears on the plaintiff's own evidence, that there has been some interruption which in its nature is permanent, the onus is on the plaintiff of proving that such interruption in fact did not continue with his acquiescence for a year: but if the interruption is in its nature fluctuating and temporary, the onus of proving that it in fact continued and was acquiesced in by the plaintiff for a year lies on the defendant. That was in *Presland v. Bingham*, 41 Ch. D. 268, where light had been interrupted by a pile of packing-cases of varying height according to the number of packing-cases the defendant happened to require to pile up at the time: and the question was whether that was an obstruction that had been acquiesced in for a year so as to constitute an interruption within the Act.

Section 5 provides:

And be it further enacted that in all actions upon the case and other pleadings wherein the party claiming may now by law allege his right generally, without averring the existence of such right from time immemorial, such general allegation shall be deemed sufficient; and if the same shall be denied, all and every the matters in this Act mentioned and provided which shall be applicable to the case shall be admissible in evidence to sustain or rebut such allegation; and that in all pleadings to actions of trespass, and in all other pleadings wherein before the passing of this Act it would have been necessary to allege the right to have existed from time immemorial, it shall be sufficient to allege the enjoyment thereof as of right by the occupiers of the tenement in respect whereof the same is claimed for and during such of the periods mentioned in this Act as may be applicable to the case, and without claiming in the name or right of the owner of the fee as is now usually done; and if the other party shall intend to rely on any proviso, exception, incapacity, disability, contract, agreement or other matter hereinbefore mentioned, or on any cause or matter of fact or of law not inconsistent with the simple fact of enjoyment, the same shall be specially alleged and set forth in answer to the allegation of the party claiming, and shall not be received in evidence on any general traverse or denial of such allegation.

This section speaks very much for itself. It simplifies the law as to pleadings, and it simplifies the pleadings themselves.

What I have to do is to state the rules that governed the pleading of prescriptive rights prior to the Act. These rules are to be found commented upon in *Chitty on Pleading*, Vol. I. pp. 393—397. Now the primary distinction to be taken is between real actions in which the right or title forms the subject of inquiry and personal actions in which damages are sought.

Now it may be stated generally that in real actions the title must be specially declared on, and pleaded and made out. Com. Dig., *Pleader*, 31. 5; Buller, N. P. 122. In personal actions, whether as to personal or real property, of course unless some interest of some kind were stated to belong to the plaintiff in the subject-matter of the suit at the time the wrong was committed, the omission would be fatal, even after verdict. The fault in the declaration would only be cured if the plea admitted the interest of the plaintiff.

But though some interest must be stated in personal actions generally, at all events as against mere wrong-doers, or persons not having any apparent colour of right, it is sufficient to declare the possession, and the title need not be specially stated.

It has always been the case that in trespass to real property a special title need not be shown in the declaration. The averment should state the trespass, and then state that the house or close in reference to which it was committed was the close of the plaintiff. That general allegation is sufficient see Com. Dig., *Pleader*, 3 M. 9. Under that evidence of a title in possession is admissible (see *Watts v. Kempe*, 2 Bulst. 288). Though there does not seem any particular reason for it, it seems at one time to have been usual in other personal actions for injury to real estate to aver the plaintiff's title specially: *e.g.* that he was seised in fee and was entitled as by prescription or grant to the right in question. But it afterwards became well established that at Common Law it was sufficient as against a mere wrong-doer to declare generally on the possession, and that by reason of such possession he was entitled to the right in question. And it became established that even against the owner of the soil such general allegation was sufficient in the declaration; but in a plea it was always necessary to allege the title specially. Thus in pleading a prescriptive right of common as a justification, the defendant was obliged to plead a seisin in fee of the land in respect of which the claim was made, and prescribe in a que estate for the right.

In pleadings under the Act the right may be declared generally where that was before allowed, and a general denial of the right would admit evidence under any head of defence contained in the Act. In pleas where it had been necessary to state the title specially, the title under the Act was to be specially stated[1].

Of course where the claim is not under the Act but at Common Law, the old Common Law rules apply except so far as they have been altered by the new rules under the Judicature Acts. Under the new rules every material fact upon which a party relies must be pleaded, so that a title so far as it is a material fact to be made out to the full must be pleaded, but not perhaps with the strict verbal accuracy required in the old days of pleading.

It must be borne in mind that this all refers merely to the requirements of form in the pleadings. At the trial it was of course necessary to adduce evidence of, and prove, all these material facts of the title despite the fact that they need not be alleged. That is of course so far as in law a title was required in the particular case. For as against a trespasser possession is a sufficient title.

The 6th section provides:

And be it further enacted that in the several cases mentioned in and provided for by this Act no presumption shall be allowed or made in favour or support of any claim upon proof of the exercise or enjoyment of the right or matter claimed for any less period of time or number of years than for such period

---

[1] As cases of interest in which these points of pleading were discussed may be cited, *Symonds v. Seaborne*, Cro. Car. 325; *Gay v. Bacchus*, 1 Showers, 17; *Strode v. Byrt*, 4 Mod. 418; *Gard v. Callard*, 6 M. & W. 69; *Dent v. Oliver*, Cro. Jac. 43; *Bailiffs of Tewkesbury v. Diston*, 6 East, 438; *Drake v. Wigglesworth*, Willes, 654, and other cases collected by Williams in his note 2 Saund. 113 a, to *Cayton v. Lethbridge*.

or number mentioned in this Act as may be applicable to the case and to the nature of the claim.

Sections 7 and 8 deal so much with the same points that it is convenient to treat of them together.

Section 7:

Provided also that the time during which any person otherwise capable of resisting any claim to any of the matters before mentioned shall have been or shall be an infant, idiot, non compos mentis, feme covert, or tenant for life, or during which any action or suit shall have been pending, and which shall have been diligently prosecuted, until abated by the death of any party or parties thereto, shall be excluded in the computation of the periods hereinbefore mentioned, except only in cases where the right or claim is hereby declared to be absolute and indefeasible.

Section 8:

Provided always and be it further enacted, that when any land or water upon, over, or from which any such way or other convenient watercourse or use of water shall have been or shall be enjoyed or derived hath been or shall be held under or by virtue of any term of life, or any term of years exceeding three years from the granting thereof, the time of the enjoyment of any such way or other matter as herein last-before mentioned, during the continuance of such term, shall be excluded in the computation of the said period of 40 years, in case the claim shall within 3 years next after the end or sooner determination of such term be resisted by any person entitled to any reversion expectant on the determination thereof.

There are several points in these two sections requiring comment. There is great difficulty in construing them together, and the difficulties seem to have arisen rather from carelessness in drafting than from any necessary difficulty in the subject itself. With regard to the classes of persons under disability, there can be little doubt that since the Married Women's Property Act, 1882, feme covert should be excluded, since the effect of that Act was to make her 'discovert'; *Lowe v. Fox*, 15 Q. B. D. 667; *Weldon v. Neal*, 1884, W. N. 153. Then with regard to the tenant for life it will be observed that the

7th section only provides for the exclusion of this period when the person otherwise capable of resisting a claim shall himself have been tenant for life; while the 8th section provides for the exclusion of the period of any tenancy for life, but that only in the case of particular classes of rights. Then with regard to the abatement of actions by death it has now been provided under the Judicature Acts, by Ord. 17, r. 1, that no cause or matter shall become abated by the death of any parties. And the subsequent rules, 2—10, provide for what is to be done in case of death of parties.

Now it is to be observed that with regard to claims under the 7th section, although the periods of disability are to be excluded in computing the prescriptive period, yet the period of indefeasibility is fixed as the extreme limit of the allowance for disabilities. Hence it may occur that where a disability has intervened, the duration of which is to be excluded in computing the primary period, but not in computing the period of indefeasibility, the longer period of indefeasibility, the 40 or 60 years as the case may be, may have elapsed before the primary period of 20 or 30 years has been concluded. This is something more than a mere curiosity arising from the peculiar manner of fixing the extreme period for disabilities, because it may well happen that if a right were claimed only by enjoyment for the 20 or 30 years the claim would fail; while if instead or in addition it had been claimed by reason of enjoyment for the 40 or 60 years, the claim would suceeed. But with regard to claims under the 8th section, the periods of disability are not restricted at all, in the computation of the longer periods.

The case stands thus: under the 7th section, which includes all rights within the Act, the periods of disability are to be excluded in computing the shorter, but not the longer periods. The 8th section provides, that with regard to the rights within it, the periods of disability are to be excluded in computing the longer periods, making no mention of the period of 20 years. It was thought, and there is a dictum of Parke, B., to that effect in *Bright v. Walker*, that the longer period would include the shorter. He then says :—" It is quite certain that an enjoyment of 40 years instead of 20, under the circumstances of this case, would have given no title against the bishop, as he might dispute the right at any time within three years after the expiration of the lease; and if the lease for life be excluded from the longer period as against the bishop it certainly must from the shorter. To so hold would have been to make the 8th section consistent, so far as possible without going contrary to express words, with the 7th. But in the subsequent case of *Park v. Skinner*, 18 Q. B. 568, it was held that in the 8th section expressio unius was exclusio alterius, and that the periods of disability were not to be excluded in reckoning the shorter periods. We have it therefore that under the 7th section the periods of disability are to be excluded in computing the shorter but not the longer periods. That proceeds upon the principle that there is an ultimate extreme limit to be fixed for disabilities. The principle which in the 8th section gives the converse result is, that though for the primary period no period of disability should be excluded, yet before the right becomes indefeasible by the lapse of the longer period, all times of disability without limit must be excluded. Either principle is equally good, and would apply equally well to both sections, and there appears no reason why both sections should not be governed by the same. Of course where one is dealing with rights coming within the 7th section exclusively no difficulty arises, but where one is dealing with rights coming equally within the 7th and 8th sections there is nothing to indicate which section is to prevail, and whether, when one is considering the short or the long period, the time of disability is to be included or excluded. It should be observed further, that section 7 applies only to a tenancy for life, not for years, while section 8 applies both to terms for life and for years.

It was thought that upon the face of the Act there was an inconsistency between the 4th section and the 7th and 8th. The 4th section requires the enjoyment to have been for a period of years next before action; while the 7th and 8th provide for the exclusion of periods of disability. If then a period of disability occurs during the period before the action, how can it be said that the enjoyment has been for the period next before action? The point arose in *Clayton v. Corby*, 2 Q. B. 813. There a life estate had intervened in the period next before action, and the question was whether a right to dig clay was established under the Act by proof of user for 25 years prior to the life estate, during the life estate, and for 6 years after the termination of the life estate continuously down to the action. It was held that the sections must be read together, and that they must be read in their strict sense, viz. that the right was to be enjoyed for 30 years next before the action, but that the period of the life tenancy was to be excluded in the calculation of the 30 years which were to be reckoned quite irrespectively of it. So that if the life tenancy be subsisting at the date of the action, the claimant must show 30 years' enjoyment prior to the beginning of the life estate : while if it be ended, the 30 years must be made up of the enjoyment before and after the life estate. It does not appear directly from this case what would be the effect supposing the enjoyment did not continue during the life estate, whether the time of the duration of the life estate is to be excluded so far as the enjoyment is concerned. And so far as the mere words of the sections are concerned, it would not appear necessary for the enjoyment to have continued during the life tenancy. Of course where the full period has elapsed prior to the life tenancy, the mere non user during the life tenancy would be immaterial except as evidence of abandonment, for which of course it would be admissible. But where the full period has not elapsed prior to the life estate, but the enjoyment has to be reckoned by adding together the periods of enjoyment before and after the life tenancy up to the action, the question arises whether, if the period of life tenancy is to be excluded, the claimant is not also to get the benefit of the exclusion and be relieved from the necessity of showing continuous enjoyment during that period. Of course, as has already been pointed out, the enjoyment must be actual and must be continuous : the only question is whether it is required to be actual and to be continuous during any longer period than that which by the Act the claimant is allowed to count in his favour. I do not find any direct authority upon the point, but Lord Denman in *Clayton v. Corby sup.*, lays stress upon the fact that the enjoyment continued during the life estate, and it may be that the fact of non-enjoyment during the period of disability would be held admissible in evidence as showing there was no actual enjoyment; though it would appear hard that the plaintiff should be required to actually enjoy during any period other than that directly mentioned by the Act.

The single easement of light is in a position of certainty owing to its having no primary period but only a period of indefeasibility after 20 years' enjoyment. After 20 years the right becomes indefeasible, therefore under section 7, periods of disability are not to be excluded: and no question can arise as to whether section 7 or section 8 is to prevail since section 8 only applies to periods of 40 years.

It would seem too that by the chance omission of rights of common and other profits in section 8, for there seems no other reason why they should not have been mentioned, no question can arise and that they come wholly under section 7. It is rather difficult to determine what the precise object of the enactment of section 8 was. One cannot help suspecting that the draftsman desired to supplement section 7 by some reference to terms of years, and proposed section 8 as a rough sketch of what he would propose: and that then it was hurriedly and without consideration included in the Act. Of course when the disability is an intervening term of years the two sections are not inconsistent. Only section 8 applies. And in cases of life tenancies section 7 alone applies where the right is not resisted within 3 years of its determination. It is only where it is so resisted that the inconsistency arises. It is worth noticing also that section 8 has been construed, so as to quiet titles and avoid litigation as much as possible. It has been held that reversion does not include a remainder. The point first arose in *Laird v. Briggs*, 16 Ch. D. 440; *on appeal*, 19 Ch. D. 22. Fry, J., thought that reversion included a remainder. The Court of Appeal, though it decided the case upon another ground and expressly left the point open, yet evidently leaned to the opposite view.

But in the subsequent case of *Symons v. Leaker*, 15 Q. B. D. 632, a divisional court was called upon to decide the point; and it held that the technical word reversion must be used in its technical sense, and could not be construed to include a remainder.

But there is still further doubt, not yet resolved, as to what rights section 8 really includes. The words are "any such way or other convenient watercourse or use of water." This is evidently an error, but as Jessel, M.R., pointed out in *Laird v. Briggs, sup.*, it is one thing to perceive that it is an error; it is another to be able to supply the proper word. He then says, p. 33, "A judge may take the view that the 8th section as it stands is so absurd that the word 'convenient' cannot stand there, but that does not quite conclude the question as to whether you can insert another word. A judge may take the view that there is sufficient in the 8th section, and some of the following (?) sections to enable them to insert another word. All I wish to say is that I think the question is open for discussion, and it must not be treated as concluded by the judgment of Fry, J., upon the point." There is some uncertainty as to what Jessel, M.R., was here referring to. As Mr Goddard says, p. 204, "This judgment is not reported at all in the Law Reports, and the *Law Journal* only says that Fry, J., when reading the section of the Act paused to say 'which word, 'convenient,' is, I understand, not unreasonably supposed to be a misprint for easement.'"

CHAPTER III.

Who may Prescribe; Who may be Prescribed against.

I HAVE now completed as fully as time will allow me the first branch of my subject. I have examined the question what time is requisite to support prescription in the various ways in which it can be claimed. I now come to deal with persons. This part of the subject naturally divides itself into two heads. (1) *Who may prescribe.* (2) *Who may be prescribed against.*

Section I.

First then, as to the persons who may prescribe. It will make this part of the subject plainer to notice here shortly the difference between a custom and a prescription. The result of both is very much the same to the person against whom they are claimed. They frequently very much resemble one another, and it may be that in some cases the aggregate number of the individuals claiming by prescription may exactly coincide with the general body who would claim by custom, if that were possible. But for all that the distinction is a real one, and has important legal consequences.

The distinction is this. A custom is local, while a prescription is personal. As Coke says, Co. Litt. 113 b: "In the Common Law a prescription, which is personal, is for the most part applyed to persons, being made in the name of a certain person and his ancestors, or those whose estate he hath; or in bodies politique or corporate and their predecessors; for as a naturall body is said to have ancestors so a body politique or corporate is said to have predecessors. And a custom, which is local, alledged in no person, but layd within some manor or other place. As taking one example for many: I. S. seised of the Mannor of D. in fee prescribed thus:—that I. S., his ancestors and all those whose estate he hath in the sayd manor, have time out of minde of man had and used to have common of pasture etc. in such a place etc. being the land of some other etc. as pertaining to the sayd manor. A copyholder of the mannor of D. doth plead, that within the same mannor there is and hath beene such a custome time out of minde of man used, that all the copyholders of the said mannor have been and used to have common of pasture etc. in such a wast of the Lord parcell of the sayd mannor D. when the person neither doth nor can prescribe but alledgeth the custome within the mannor. But both to customes and prescriptions these two things are incidents inseparable, viz. possession or usage and time."

Prescription then must be alleged by the claimant as having been enjoyed by himself and his ancestors or by himself and those whose estate he hath, which latter is called prescription in a que estate. In the light of the shortening of time under the doctrine of the modern lost grant and the Prescription Act we may now add that it may be claimed by a man himself as having been enjoyed for the proper period.

Now the claim in gross by a man for enjoyment by himself and his ancestors is very infrequent, at any rate in the case of private individuals, though more frequent by corporations. However, there can be no doubt that as claimed by private individuals it is good in law. It is exceedingly rare in modern times. I have only been able to find two cases in which it has ever been made—the one a claim at Common Law which succeeded, and the other a claim under the Prescription Act which failed.

The first is the case of *Welcome v. Upton*, 6 M. and W. 536.

There in trespass for taking the plaintiff's cattle in an open field called P. and S. field and impounding them the defendant pleaded first that T. B. and his ancestors had been immemorially used and accustomed to have for themselves and their heirs and assigns the sole and several pasturage in 217 acres of P. and S. field in gross for all his and their cattle from the 4th of Sept. to the 5th of April: that T. B. in 1755 by indenture granted

the said pasturage to S. B. and his heirs and assigns for ever:
that T. B. (who claimed by descent from S. B.) in 1836 demised
the said pasturage to the defendant who seised the plaintiff's
cattle because they were depasturing on the said 217 acres.

It was held that the right of pasturage alleged in the pleas
was capable of being granted away and did not necessarily
descend to the heir of the grantor. And that the plea was
good.

It had before that been decided in the cases of *Hoskins v.
Robins*, Pollexfen, 13; 2 Wms. Saund. 320, and *Potter v. North*,
1 Ventr. 385, that a party may prescribe to take the sole and
several herbage[1]. But those two cases when examined were
both cases of a prescription in a que estate.

The other modern case of a claim by prescription by a man
and his ancestors is that of *Shuttleworth v. Le Fleming and
others*, 19 C. B., N. S. 687. That was a claim to a right of free
fishing in gross under the Prescription Act by reason of 60 years'
enjoyment. The question was argued very fully, but it was
decided that the Prescription Act did not apply to easements or
profits a prendre in gross. Montague Smith, J., in delivering
the judgment of the Court, said :—" The language of the 1st
section may be sufficiently large to include some rights in
gross...we think, however, that the 1st section ought not to
be read alone, but must be construed with reference to the
other provisions of the Act.

"The 2nd section relates to easements and to watercourses.
We think this section refers to easements properly so-called,
and to rights which are in some way appurtenant to a dominant
tenement...But the 5th section, which relates to pleading,
seems to us to give a key to the true construction of the Act."

The whole principle of this section assumes a dominant
tenement and an enjoyment of the right by the occupiers of it.

It is true that there are older cases where a right in gross

---

[1] It is worthy of remark in passing
that the report of the case in Pollexfen's Reports is misleading. It appears
that he argued the case for the defendant and lost. He afterwards published
reports, and thinking his argument
good, inserted it in his Reports. It
has often been mistaken for the judgment of the Court, which was however
the other way.

was claimed successfully by individuals not incorporated, and that though the predecessors in whose right they claimed were not their progenitors and had no blood connexion of any kind. But it appears that though a succession through blood was not absolutely essential, yet some sort of a succession or perpetuity of the predecessors and the claimant was required.

Thus it was held that a sergeant-at-law may prescribe that he and all sergeants have used to be impleaded only by writ original. In that case (see Vin. Abr. p. 256) a Bill of Debt was brought against a sergeant-at-law who said that he came to the Bar to plead and minister matter for his client, and bill does not lie against him; "and after he said that he is a sergeant-at-law, and that he and all sergeants-at-law time out of mind have been impleaded by writ original and not by bill, and demanded judgment if the Court will take conusance. The plaintiff demurred. Per Brian, 'You cannot prescribe; for you are not incorporated.'" But it was held, several may prescribe who are not incorporated, as officer of the Court shall prescribe in privilege, &c.

See too Br. Abr. *Prescript.* Pl. 72.

I take the passage shortly as given above because in the *Year Book*, 11 E. IV. 2. 6, it is too long to set out at length. But the question of the privileges of officers of the Court as attorneys and clerks in Chancery was there discussed, and it was held that an attorney may prescribe, that he and all attorneys, have used to have privilege, &c.

But the decision in these cases though interesting historically is not of much value as establishing any principle with regard to prescription, since the question was not simply one of prescription, but was mixed up with the other considerations of the privileges of officers of the Court, and that being so, one cannot tell how far they may have been considered as analogous to a corporation, or how far the royal privilege may have carried them. So it is said (Br. Abr. *Prescription*, Pl. 4, citing 20 H. VI. 8) that a man may allege a custom Quod quilibet Capitalis Justiciarius de Banco pro tempore existens has used dare quodlibet officium of the Court. But as to this, of course the previous remarks equally apply.

That, however, some kind of a succession by right and not a mere tenure of an office at will is required seems to follow from these cases.—In the *Year Book*, 42 E. III. 5, it is adjudged that a sheriff cannot prescribe that he and all those who have been sheriffs have been seised of a certain gift at every town— for the sheriff is chosen by the king every year and removable at the king's will.

So again (Br. Abr. *Prescription*—citing 32 H. VI. 31), in debt it was awarded that the sexton of an abbey cannot prescribe that he and his predecessors, sextons of the abbey of B., have been parsons of the said abbey in B., and have im- pleaded and been impleaded time out of mind ; for a sexton cannot prescribe, and grant to him by the king shall not serve his successors ; *for he has no succession*, quaere of himself ? For it seems that he is a monk, and therefore a dead person in the law.

Another peculiar case of a claim of prescription in gross, which also would fail in addition to the reason therein given for its failure, by reason of its not being any succession as of right is to be found in 20 H. VI. 18. See Br. Abr. *Prescription*, Pl. 4, Vin. Abr. p. 257.

There upon scire facias to repeal letters patent of the king of an office in Ireland against T. N. because the plaintiff had other letters patent of it of elder date the defendant said, that the land of Ireland is and time out of mind has been a land severed from the realm of England, and ruled and governed by the laws and customs there, and that the lords there of the king's council have used in the absence of the king to choose a justice, who has power to pardon and punish all felonies and trespassers, and to assemble a Parliament by advice of the Lords and Commonalty and make statutes, and alleged how a Parlia- ment was summoned by which it was enacted that those who have offices there shall be resident upon it by a certain day, or otherwise shall forfeit his office, and that the plaintiff was officer, and did not come by the day, by which the office was void, and was granted to the defendant. The other demurred upon the plea, and by some the prescription is contrary to reason, and is also one that that would bind the king (poit lier le roy), and therefore ill. But per Fortescue the prescription is void, and is in the king and not to those in Ireland: as chancellor of England, who is only at will, prescribes to have presentation to all benefices of the king under a certain sum, and that Statutes of England as to 10ths, 15ths, etc. do not bind Ireland, because it is severed and does not come to Parliament, therefore quaere legem.

On the other hand the following two cases seem exceptions, and at any rate not readily reconcilable with the foregoing principle.

See Br. Abr. *Prescript.* Pl. 37, 21 H. VII. 16, 6 Vin. Abr. 257.

An under-sheriff prescribed that he and all under-sheriffs of the county have used to have so much for bar fees. And this was admitted good.

So again Br. Abr. *Prescription,* Pl. 94, 2 E. IV.; 17 Vin. Abr. 257.

A prior dative and removable prescribed to implead and be impleaded and to answer and be answered time out of mind, and held a good prescription. But with regard to the sheriff in the later case, Vin. Abr. 262, where a vicar libelled in the Spiritual Court for a stipend of £4 per annum, claiming it by prescription, a prohibition was moved for upon the ground that none can claim a stipend by prescription but a corporation or body politic. Holt, J., so held, but said that a sheriff though removable at the will of the king might claim a fee as incident of his office, *i.e.* he cannot claim a fee by prescription, but he while holding the office may claim the fee as an incident of the office. It would seem therefore that for practical purposes the sheriff was no worse off in this respect than his under-sheriff.

So much then for prescriptions in gross by single individuals. Such prescriptions by Corporations are very much more frequent. Thus in *Johnson v. Barnes,* L. R., 7 C. P. 592, and on appeal L. R., 8 C. P. 527, the Corporation of Colchester claimed by immemorial usage an exclusive right of pasturage; they claimed a right of common, and though the Court of First Instance held, as the law no doubt was, that a right of common is extinguished by a release of any part of the land subject to it, yet it also held that this was a peculiar right of common, being granted to the Corporation in gross out of the land *and each atom thereof*, so that there was power to release any part without extinguishing the right of common as to the rest; but the Court of Appeal having regard to a similar case of *Rex v. Churchill*, 4 B. and C. 750, held that the claim as a right of common was an erroneous description, and that what they were really claiming was a sola vestura or exclusive right of pasturage, and held that good, in lands near the town for commonable animals levant and couchant within the borough from Lammas to Candlemas. The right had been in several instances for value released to the owners of part of the lands, and in some cases the right had been conveyed to strangers. This was held a good claim by prescription in gross. The Court expressly decided that it was a claim in gross by deciding the point that the levancy and couchancy of the animals was a mere method of regulating the number of animals that could be placed on the land in exercise of the right, and had no reference to the claim being made as appendant or appurtenant to the land owned by the Corporation.

With regard, however, to claims of this kind there is one point of some uncertainty. There are cases where claims by prescription are made by inhabitants, and that where the inhabitants are not incorporated. Of course a corporation can go by what name it chooses, and if the inhabitants of any place are incorporated by that name, they have all the rights of a corporation: and it is to be observed that inhabitants though not incorporated can take by grant from the Crown, and are to that extent incorporated: Dyer, 100; *Lockwood v. Wood*, 6 Q. B. 50; *Willingale v. Maitland*, 12 Jur. N. S. 932.

Now it was decided in *Gateward's Case*, 6 Rep. 59 b, that inhabitants when unincorporated cannot prescribe for a right of common or any profit a prendre. So that where cases occur of claims of this nature by inhabitants, they are to be explained as either due to mere popular language or to the fact that where there is a corporation enjoying such a right the inhabitants who are tenants of the Corporation enjoy the right also, but not qua inhabitants, it is of course qua tenants of the corporation. Thus Br. Abr. *Prescrip.* 28 : 15 E. IV. 29 ; Vin. Abr. 256, it was agreed that the Mayor and citizens of Coventry may prescribe for them *and their inhabitants and not otherwise.*

But there are cases where inhabitants alone, unincorporated, have claimed to prescribe, not to rights of common or other profits a prendre, but to easements, or to be discharged, and the claim has been held good. It does not appear whether these claims were claims in gross or in a que estate, and I think the explanation may possibly be that these claims were in respect of easements appurtenant to the land of the inhabitants so claiming. Thus Br. Abr. *Prescrip.* pl. 76, 18 E. IV. 3.

"Prescription may be that the usage of the Vill of D. has been time out of mind that the inhabitants have had way over the land of the plaintiff to the church, or that they have been quit of toll at the Mill; and that inhabitants may prescribe in easement contra in profit apprender out of another's land: per Pigot, which was not contradicted." Vin. Abr. 256.

So again inhabitants, unless they are incorporated, cannot prescribe to have profit in the soil of another, but in matters of easement only, as in a way to a church: so in matters of discharge: as to be discharged of toll or tithes, or in a modus decimandi: but not in matters of interest, as *e.g.* putting stalls on another's land without paying, see *Lockwood v. Wood,* 6 Q. B. 31, 62 seq.

Smith v. Gatewood, 6 Rep. 59, 3 Cro. Jac. 152.

This case is one of so much interest, that I shall need no further excuse for setting it out at some length.

In trespass by Robert Smith against Stephen Gateward gent, quare clausum fregit in the Vill of Horsington by pasturing cattle there, defendant pleaded a custom for every inhabitant of the ancient Vill of Stixwold ratione commorantiae to have common of pasture in the place in question. And pleaded that he praed' tempore quo fuit et adhuc est commorans et inhabitans in the said town of Stixwold in an ancient house in S. praed', and so justified. Upon which the plaintiff did demur in law. And it was unanimously resolved by all the Justices of the Common Pleas that the custom was against law for several reasons.

(1)   That the claim was not for any common known to the law.

(2)   That a man who had no interest in the house could have no interest in the common.

(3)   A custom can only extend to that which hath certainty and continuance.

(4)   It would be against the nature and quality of a common, for every common may be suspended or extinguished, but such a common would be so incident to the person that no person certain could extinguish it, but as soon as he who released it removed the new inhabitant should have it.

(5)   If the law should allow such common the law would give an action or remedy for it; but he who claims it as inhabitant can have no action for it.

(6)   That an inhabitant had no sufficient interest to enable him to plead in the name of the owner of the fee.

(7)   No improvement could be made in any wastes if such common should be allowed.

But two differences are taken and agreed by the whole Court.

(1)   Between a charge in the soil of another and a discharge in his own soil.

(2)   Between an interest or profit to be taken or had in another's soil.   And therefore a custom that every inhabitant of a town hath paid a modus decimandi to the parson in discharge of their tithes is good; for they claim not a charge or profit apprender in the soil of another, but a discharge in their own land: so of a custom that every inhabitant of such a town shall have a way over such land either to the church or market, &c., that is good, for it is but an easement and no profit; and a way or passage may well follow the person, and no such inconvenience as in the case at bar.

(8)   It is resolved that copyholders in fee or for life, may by custom of the manor have common in the demesnes of the Lord of the Manor.

It seems also that the custom ought to have been in any case alleged as a custom of the town of Horsington and not of Stixwold.

This case has since its decision been the leading authority for the proposition that inhabitants unless incorporated, cannot by custom or prescription establish a right to any profit in alieno solo.

The passage in this report which has been translated " So none that hath no interest, if it be but at will, ought to have common; but by good pleading he may enjoy it," makes Lord Coke appear to consider that rights of common depend entirely upon having good counsel. But the passage is evidently a mistranslation which has been pointed out and corrected by Mr Joshua Williams in his book upon commons, p. 7. The translation he gives there is :—"So there is none that hath any interest, though it be but at will, and who ought to have common, but by good pleading he may enjoy it," *i.e.* a person who is merely tenant at will, and as tenant at will has a right of common, may enjoy his right by good pleading, *i.e.* by pleading in the name of the tenant in fee simple.

The distinction there taken between a profit and an easement has since been many times upheld, see *Fitch v. Rawling*, 2 H. B. 395, where a custom for all inhabitants of a parish to play at all kinds of lawful sports and pastimes in the close of A at all seasonable times of the year at their free will and pleasure, was held good.

See too *Bell v. Wardell*, Willes, 202.

Gateward's case came under discussion in the case of *Grimstead v. Marlowe*, 4 T. R. 717, where it was again held that a custom to take a profit in alieno solo is bad, such a right only being claimable by prescription.

In another plea, the right was claimed by a custom for every occupier of a messuage or land within the parish of Leatherhead &c. It was then attempted to distinguish Gateward's case on the ground that there the right was claimed by inhabitants simpliciter, and the same in the cases of *Weekly v. Wildman*, 1 Ld. Raym. 405. *Selby v. Robinson*, 2 T. R. 758.

But it was held that there was no distinction upon that ground, because in this case though the word inhabitants was not used, yet the claim was substantially the same, being a claim by custom and not a claim by prescription by the occupier and his predecessors in title.

In *Grimstead v. Marlowe*, Buller, J., read a note of *Hardy v. Hollyday* from one of Lord Chief Justice King's MSS., which contained the following claim:—

"That Cambridge is an ancient borough and there is a certain ancient laudable custom from time whereof, &c., that every tenant and inhabitant of and in any messuage within the said borough has and &c. common of pasture for beasts levant and couchant, &c.

Upon demurrer the Court held it bad, but said that he might have prescribed in the corporation, that the town of Cambridge was a corporation time out of mind, and that the corporation for *themselves* and *every burgess* had a common, &c., as in *Melcher v. Spateman*, 1 Saund. 343.

But where the party pleading is a stranger to the title as in *Starr v. Rooksby*, Salk. 335, he may declare on the custom. *Case*, for that he was possessed of a close adjoining to the defendant's and the tenants and occupiers of the defendant's close had time out of mind used to repair the fences, &c., and held good, because it was impossible for the plaintiff who was a stranger to set forth the particular estate, interest and title of the defendant.

Prescription in a que estate.

I now come to the second division of this branch of my subject—prescription by a man and those whose estate he has—or as it is called shortly prescription in a que estate, being taken from the Norman French tous ceux que estate il ad.

It was held in the case of *Dorney v. Cashford*, Salk. 363, that though the tenant for years cannot prescribe in a que estate because of the imbecility of his interest, yet as against a wrongdoer he may allege that as tenant for years of a house he had and of right ought to have the way in question. In *Bean v. Bloom*, 2 Black. 228; De Grey, C.J., and Cur. say :—

"The same rights may be claimed either by custom or prescription—one is local, the other personal; and the difference lies in the mode of claim, suited to the difference of the claimants. When the claimant has a weak and temporary estate, he cannot claim in his own right, but must have recourse either to the place and claim a custom there; *or if he prescribes in a que estate it must be under cover of the tenant in fee.*" I quote the rest of the judgment because it was delivered with reference to Gateward's case, cited in argument. "The case of a copyholder claiming common by custom is a strong instance. So occupiers of houses may set up a custom to cut turves; *occupiers of lands may by custom claim a right in alieno solo; though inhabitants cannot,* because inhabiting is too vague a description, and extends to many others besides the actual occupiers of houses and lands. But in the present case this claim is not set up by the plaintiff merely as occupier of a house : it is claimed as annexed and appurtenant to a right of common which is admitted to be sufficiently set forth; it is merely a beneficial circumstance connected by custom to the acknowledged right of common. He claims the right to cut rushes not as occupier but as commoner : and doubtless a commoner may set up a custom that such and such rights are an appendage to his common."

There are some further remarks upon the question of the alternative claim by custom and by prescription in the case of *Day v. Savage,* Hobart, 86.

"But yet common for copyholders in the lord's soil is allowed to be pleaded by custom for necessity sake, whereas on the soil of another it must be laid by prescription in the lord, and yet the nature of both is a prescription."

The necessity for pleading in the name of the tenant in fee is again laid down in Dyer, 71 a.

"It is observable in our books that a tenant at will or for years or life cannot prescribe in their own names to have common from the weakness of their estates, but ought to prescribe in the name of the lord as appears from *Chaworth's case,* 9 H. VI. 62 and 18 E. IV. 3, pl. 15."

So in that pleader's manual of the period, the "Doctrina Placitandi, ou l'art et science de Bon Pleading," printed in 1677, under the head prescription we find the rule :—

"Nul poit prescribe mais que ad fee, et touts autres estates derive hors del fee come lessee pur ans, vie ou al volunt, doient prescriber en il que ad le fee."

See too 15 E. IV. 29, pl. 7, and *Holbetts v. Warner*, 2 Rolle's Rep. 288.

A tenant at will must get his lord, whom, and whom alone, the question affects, since the tenancy is but at will, to assert the right, and then the tenant at will may by good pleading enjoy his right. The difference is that as against anyone but his lord, a tenant at will may by proper pleading enjoy his right, while tenants of other descriptions have such a right, as by good pleading, and possibly nolente volente, their lord, because it does not appear quite certain that the leave of the lord had to be obtained to use his name, they may assert against others. Of course none save a tenant in fee could prescribe against the lord since the prescription being in his name, would not lie against himself. To this inability of a tenant at will to assert his right, there is the one exception adverted to in the case of *Bean v. Bloom, supra*, that is the case of the copyholder who is of course but a tenant at will of the lord. Now of course if a copyholder was claiming a right of common in the lands of any other than his lord, he was bound to assert it in accordance with this rule of pleading. But supposing, as would usually be the case, the copyholder was desiring to assert a claim over the wastes of his lord, then of course a prescription in the name of the lord was impossible for reasons both technical and practical. In such a case the copyholders were allowed, as said in *Day v. Savadge, supra*, to plead their right by alleging a custom within the manor, for necessity sake. So that with regard to a claim over the wastes of the lord a copyholder was so far in a better position than a tenant at will with regard to other claims. Though practically the lord might be trusted not to be negligent in asserting his own rights. As is said in *Pearce v. Bacon*, Cro. Eliz. 390, "Though in ancient time they were accounted only as tenants at will and so might not prescribe against their lord, yet now they be accounted in an high regard, and may therefore prescribe against their lord."

An apparently different reason is given for allowing copyholders to prescribe by alleging a custom in the manor in the case of *Taverner v. Lord Cromwell*, Cro. Eliz. 353.

In the case of *Honeywood v. Husbands*, Cro. Eliz. 153, the question arose of how a tenant for years ought to plead when he had taken his demise from the tenant for life and the remainderman jointly. There was a difference of opinion between Gaudy, J., and Wray, C.J., and the point does not seem to have been settled.

That case seems therefore to make it necessary to claim the right in the name of the person who last had the whole fee. The dictum of Wray, C.J., in the above case is however supported by what was said by Noy, A.-G., in *The Inhabitants of Egham's Case*, Jo. 275, 8 Car. in Itin. Windsor. There the inhabitants of Egham and all the towns in Surrey joined in a claim to cut down all the coppices at their pleasure, and to have common for all cattle commonable, and Common of Turbary, and made title by prescription: and Noy, A.-G., said that they ought not to have joined in one claim.

It seems, however, that this rule against a joint claim was not allowed to work any real injustice or deprive any one of his rights if he could not otherwise assert them. For it seems to have been relaxed in every case where some technical or other reason required it. Thus tenants in ancient demesne for whom jointly the king would have been the lord to make claim, were allowed to make a joint claim for common, &c., because the king could not come into the Courts and claim for them. Jo. 276 in S. C. Vin. Abr. p. 258 n.

So, too, though of course a lord when claiming for his copyholders made a claim on behalf of several jointly, yet he might only claim in respect of such as were his tenants, and the freehold of whose land was in law in him, but not for any others. *Ibid.*

And the lord could not claim on behalf of any of the freeholders, even in conjunction with the copyholders: nor could the freeholders claim jointly, but each of them was bound to put in a separate claim. *Ibid.*

Where, however, the several persons making a claim form a body aggregate the claim is allowed. Thus in *Dickman v.*

Allen, 2 Vent., Hil. Anno 1 and 2 W. and M. in C. B. in a prescription in the Provost and Scholars of King's College, Cambridge, the claim was allowed, the report concluding thus, "Nota here a prescription is laid in a body aggregate in a que estate, but that was held to be well enough because for a thing appurtenant to the manor."

See too 1 *Inst.* 121 a, Bellewe, 140 B.

Slackman v. West, Cro. Jac. 673, was a case of an action on the case by a lessee from a corporation—the governor and the poor of the Hospital of the Holy Trinity in Greenwich; against the defendant for having erected a gate across a way claimed by the plaintiff under the said corporation. It was there objected that the claim was bad as the lessee could not show the que estate without showing how it was held by deed. But the Court overruled the objection "because the action is brought by the lessee for years who hath not the deed; and it is but a conveyance to the action which is grounded upon the disturbance done to him in possession; but if he had claimed rent or common in gross, which cannot pass without deed it had been otherwise. For there he could not show que estate without showing the deed how he came by the estate.

To much the same effect is the case of *Lawson v. Hare*, 2 Vent. 74, which goes to show that where a man is seised of property, and he claims by prescription in a que estate some right, the title to which is put in issue, but not his title to the estate, then he need not produce the deed granting to him the property in respect of which he so claims.

It would be possible to pursue this subject of the form in which the claim must be alleged much further, as there is much interesting matter about it in the old reports and year books. But a due regard to proportion requires it to be left here.

The rule making it necessary to prescribe in the name of the owner of the fee prevented any question that might have arisen as to whether the claim when established, *e.g.* by a tenant for years, would enure for the benefit of the owner of the fee, or whether it was only established for the benefit of the tenant for years so establishing it. I cannot find out whether when the doctrine of the modern lost grant was introduced, it was still necessary in all cases to prescribe in the name of the owner of the fee. It is not quite easy to see how in certain cases, upon principle, it can have been requisite, since the very theory that a grant had been made immediately prior to the 20 years of which user was shown seems to preclude any such necessity—the theory being that the grant was made to the actual claimant. But then supposing him to have been a mere tenant for years one would have thought that the question would have arisen, whether the grant was to be held a grant for good and aye or only a grant during the term. The grant certainly seems to have been held to be a grant for good and enured to the reversioner ; so that whether it was necessary or not to plead in the name of the owner of the fee, that rule certainly had its effect in making the right to be established for his benefit. The prescriptive right was not gained at all unless it was gained so as to be good against everybody, including the owner of the fee. And of course under the Prescription Act (see section 5) the right is established for the owner of the fee. For although it is there provided that it shall be sufficient to allege the enjoyment as of right by the occupiers of the tenement in respect whereof the same is claimed, it also provides that it shall not be necessary to claim in the name or right of the owner of the fee. And although that proviso taken by itself is ambiguous, and might mean that the occupier might claim a right to exist during his term only, yet read in view of the general scope of the Act, and by what has been said before on the same section about avowing the existence of the right from time immemorial, it clearly means that the right shall be gained for the owner of the fee.

The rule at Common Law requiring a tenant to prescribe in the name of the owner of the fee, had another double effect in this way—it prevented a tenant from acquiring a right in the land of his lord, whether occupied by the lord, since he could not prescribe against himself: or held by another tenant at will, since the lord could not prescribe against his tenant at will. This would not extend to the case of a tenant for years since apparently the lord could prescribe in a proper case against a tenant for years, but the point does not seem to have been decided at Common Law, because in early times there were no holdings long enough to raise a prescription. In the same case, however, of two tenants holding under the same lord, under the Prescription Act the result seems to be rather different. It is true as regards easements generally under that Act, the law is not altered. The question seems at first to have been adverted to in *Daniel v. Anderson*, 31 L. J. Ch. 610, where Kindersley, V.-C., after laying down that a tenant still, since his possession is that of his landlord, cannot acquire an easement against his landlord, goes on to say, "Whatever may be the rights of one tenant against another the owner remains where he was, and therefore you cannot talk of any easement acquired by him or vesting at all, for whatever rights *one tenant may have against another*, it is only as between them as tenants."

See too *Sturges v. Bridgman*, 11 Ch. D. 885.

The question came up for decision in *Bright v. Walker*, 1 C. M. and R. 211, where it was held that one lessee for lives could not acquire an easement under the Prescription Act against another lessee for lives under the same lessor. Baron Parke in giving judgment in that case says: "We think that by the Statute such a qualified right is not given by an enjoyment of 20 years. For in the first place the Statute is for the shortening of the time of *prescription:* and if the periods in it are to be deemed new times of prescription it must have been intended that the enjoyment for those periods should give a good title against all, *for titles by immemorial prescription are absolute and valid against all.* They are such as absolutely bind the fee in the land. And in the next place the Statute nowhere contains any intimation that there are to be different classes of rights, qualified and absolute—valid as to some persons, and invalid as to others. From hence we are led to conclude that an enjoyment of 20 years, if it give not a good title against all, gives no good title at all. This view of the case derives confirmation from the 7th section... This section, it is to be observed, in express terms excludes the time that the person (who is capable of resisting the claim to the way) is tenant for life... During the period of a tenancy for life the exercise of an easement will not affect the fee; in order to do that there must be that period of enjoyment *against* an owner of the fee."

It would seem that although qualified easements of that kind, enjoyable only during a term, were not possible under claims of prescription from time of legal memory, or as there decided generally under the Prescription Act, yet that under the doctrine of modern lost grant the case was rather different. Such claims were of course naturally infrequent; and of course no supposed grant by a termor or tenant for life could have any efficiency as against the person entitled in reversion; yet it appears that in a proper case a jury might have found a grant by an owner of a limited interest, to endure only during such limited interest. Thus in *Bright v. Walker, supra*, Parke, B., says "of course nothing in the Statute will prevent the operation of an actual grant by one lessee to another, proved by the deed itself, or upon proof of its loss, by secondary evidence; *nor prevent the jury from taking the possession into consideration with other circumstances as evidence of a grant which they may still find to have been made, if they are satisfied that it was made in point of fact.*" By the last sentence, nothing more is meant than merely to state the doctrine of the lost grant, viz. that the circumstances are such that it ought to be presumed. This appears from what has been said higher up (p. 221) in the same case.

" Before the Statute this possession would indeed have been evidence to support a plea or claim by a *non-existing grant* by the termor in the locus in quo to the termor under whom the plaintiff claims, though such a claim was by no means a matter of ordinary occurrence; and in practice the usual course was to state a grant by an owner in fee to an owner in fee."

But though it is true generally of the Prescription Act that a tenant cannot acquire a right by prescription against another tenant of the same landlord, yet this does not seem to be the case with regard to easements of light, which are specially provided for by section 3.

In the case of *Frewen v. Phillips*, 11 C. B., N. S. 449, it was held that where there were two tenants holding under leases from the same landlord, and one of them had enjoyed an access of light without interruption over the land of the other for 20 years he could prevent the other from obstructing his light, though at the end of the terms (which began at the same time and were to end at the same time) such right might be extinguished by unity of ownership. But Blackburn, J., at any rate evidently thought (see p. 453) that if the reversions had by sale during the tenancies come into different hands, the right to unobstructed light would survive. So that the decision actually is nothing more than this, that although two tenants hold under one lord that does not prevent one of them from acquiring a right indefeasible (at all events in case the reversions come into different hands) but which will of course be extinguished by unity of possession. The Court certainly was alive to the difficulties that might arise from the decision, and the case does not decide what would have been the result supposing the servient tenement had come into the hands of the lord before the dominant tenement, or supposing only one of the reversions and not both, as there assumed, had been granted away.

Of course there are cases in which such rights as are the subject of prescription (and therefore of necessity the subject also of grant) are claimed as only to last for a certain period, as *e.g. Davis v. Morgan*, 4 B. and C. 8, when a right to divert water from a river to a well for 99 years is mentioned; yet all such cases are cases of express grant and have nothing whatever to do with prescription.

SECTION II.

Having now treated at some length of the question who may prescribe, I come now to consider: *Who may be prescribed against: or who is bound by a prescription.*

Under this head one consideration is, who, of persons having successive interests, are bound by a prescription: the other consideration is what kinds of people are, or rather for convenience it is best to take it, what kinds of people are not bound by a prescription. The curious thing is that almost all the authority there is upon the first point is modern, while that upon the second is comparatively ancient. The reason why no question arose as to the first point is that until the change in the nature of prescription was made, whereby it was no longer necessary to show an user from the time of legal memory, no question could arise as to whether a reversioner was bound : when however it was made requisite to show only a 20 years user, it might easily be that a reversionary estate might never here come into possession during that time, and the question was whether a reversioner under such circumstances was bound.

With regard to claims of user from the time of legal memory it is conceivable that such questions might have arisen. But it must not be forgotten that in addition to the length of time there were other reasons rendering such questions improbable. The population was very much less : land was not so much distributed ; houses were further apart, so that the numerous instances in which claims arise at the present day, particularly with regard to light, are entirely due to modern conditions. At any rate as a matter of fact these questions do not seem to have arisen.

Now in treating of who may prescribe I have, of necessity, travelled over a good deal of the ground that belongs equally to this head. I have shown that claims from the time of legal memory bind the owner of the fee or bind nobody : that claims by modern lost grant apparently could not be established for a limited period only, but when established were good in perpetuity and bound the reversioner: that under the Prescription Act, except in cases of claims to light, which might be established by one tenant against another, no claim was binding unless it was binding upon everybody. Upon this latter point, express provision is made for the case of reversioners by section 8, which provides that if the reversioner resists the continuance of the right within 3 years from the time when the reversion falls in, the intermediate time is not to be reckoned in favour of the person asserting the right.

Now there are certain people who cannot be bound by a prescription. Thus as illustrating the necessity of a succession

of some kind in order to establish a right, we find in a case in
the year book, 11 H. VII. 13, pl. 8, a distinction taken between
strangers, who cannot be bound by a prescription of the lord,
and tenants of the manor who can. It is true this looks
more like a custom than a prescription, but it is one of those
cases where a custom is allowed in aid of a prescription.

In that case the lord sued for £3. 0s. 9d. for pound breach,
alleging a custom that the lord had always had that sum
for pound breach.

But it was held bad, for "semble a touts les Justices que
l' prescr' de custome n'est bon a lier chescun estranger, p̃tant
q̃ il ne poit av̂ loyal commencement: mais si le custome fuit
que chescun tenât q̃ tient del manoir enfreint le pound il
payera £3. 0s. 9d. cest bon custome p̃ ĉ q̃ il poit av̂ loial
commencement, car le sñr poit doñ les tenements a teñ del
m̃r p̃ tiels services."

So again in Y. B. ed. Pike in M. R. series, Pasch. 13 E. III.
p. 228, Vin. Abr. 258, it is said that the lord cannot prescribe
against his villeins, nor his tenant at will. Of course this
only applies to asserting a prescription and not then to the
case of copyholders where a custom might be alleged in aid
of the right. One reason of it of course is the inability of
a man to prescribe against himself: since as regards the estate
of these tenants at will the lord was himself the representative
at law. But the true reason of it seems to be that in these
cases no prescription was required, and therefore was not
allowed. The lord could turn out the tenant at will if he
objected and there was really no injustice, since it might
well be that the lord only let in tenants at will upon those
terms.

Brooke, Abr., *Customs*, pl. 52, gives no reasons but simply
says "ne le seignior ne puit prescriber v̂s les villeins ne
les tenants a volunt."

We have it then that any tenants who had not estates
in fee must prescribe in the name of the lord, subject to
the exception in favour of copyholders.

But the reason of the rule does not apply to the converse
case. The lord might prescribe against his tenants. As to

tenants in fee the question does not arise. As to the copyholders, one class of tenants at will, it is immaterial whether
they be treated as copyholders, and subject to any custom
of the manor, or as coming under the ordinary designation
of tenants at will. In the latter case we are told the lord
could not prescribe. But that was because he could enforce
his right without prescription: he could silence any objection
by turning out the objector.

As regards tenants for life or years, though for the cause
before stated they could not prescribe against the lord, that
afforded no reason why he should not prescribe against them.
He could perfectly well allege that they and those whose
estate they had had always held it subject to the right;
and there was nothing to prevent the supposition that each
of the predecessors of the tenant had received his land only
upon those terms. The case of *Anstye v. Fawkener*, Cro. E. 446,
is somewhat in point. It was as follows:—Replevin: defendant
avows for damage feasant. Plaintiff justifies for that he had a
close adjoining defendant's close; and that the defendant and
all the occupiers of the said close from time whereof &c. had
used to repair the fences between the closes and for not
sufficient enclosing his beasts entered...moved in arrest of
judgment that the prescription that *every occupier* &c. is
too general, for tenant at will, or at sufferance or a disseisor
are occupiers.

Walmsley. "True it is the prescription is not good; for this
inclosure is a charge upon the land: and they who are only
occupiers, as a disseisor, tenant at will or sufferance cannot
charge the land therewith: but it ought to have been that
he and all those whose estate &c. But such a prescription
to pay so much in discharge of tithes by the occupiers of
lands, hath been allowed to be good; for that goes in discharge
and for the benefit of the land, and tithes arise upon the
occupying the land. But yet in regard that issue is taken
upon this prescription and a verdict hath found it, this is not
any cause for staying judgment but it is aided by the Statute
of Jeofails."

Hence it appears that just as inhabitants, there being no

succession, cannot prescribe in matters of charge though they can in matters of discharge (*Gateward's case*), so for like reason it is not good to allege that every occupier has done something which is a charge upon the land, and in any case such a charge would only be good during the term, which is determinable at any time. But every body who is in occupation is an occupier whether he be tenant in fee or no, and hence some occupiers can be prescribed against in matters of charge, if they are got at in the right way. Positive prescriptive liabilities are generally in the nature of prescriptions in a que estate. Occupiers of premises may be bound by reason of their tenure, and so far as the tenure goes, to perform certain acts. Thus Coke, 2nd Inst. p. 700, says, " Some persons spirituall or temporall, incorporate or not incorporate, are bound to repaire bridges ratione tenurae suae terrarum &c. Some ratione praescriptionis tantum. Ratione tenurae by reason that they and those whose estate they have in the lands are bound in respect thereof to repaire the same; but they which have lands on the one side of the bridge, or on the other or on both, are not bound of common right to repaire the same...ratione praescriptionis tantum herein there is a diversity between bodies politick or corporate, spirituall or temporall, and naturall persons. For bodies politicke or corporate, spirituall or temporall, may be bound by usage and prescription only, because they are locall and have a succession perpetuall: but a naturall person cannot be bound by act of his ancester without a lien or binding and assets." Thus *R. v. Inhabitants of Sheffield*, 2 T. R. 106, the township was held liable to repair highways within the township.

So in *Keighley's Case*, 10 Rep. 139:—it was held that though a man may be bound to repair a sea wall yet he has not failed of his duty if he keeps it of ordinary strength, and an extraordinary tide destroys it. Though *R. v. Leigh*, 10 A. and E. 398, is an authority for saying that the prescription may even in such a case compel him to repair. See too *Hudson v. Tabor*, 2 Q. B. Div. 290. As to pleading in such cases see *Rider v. Smith*, 3 T. R. 766.

That occupiers may be prescribed against for matters that

lay a burden or charge on the lands they possess appears from *Gunter v. More*, 17 Car. 2, C. B., where in an action on the case it was held a good count that the plaintiff had been three years last in occupation of such a pasture, and that defendant occupied such another close, and that omnes occupatores of the defendant's close did use to shut the gates. So in *R. v. Bucknall*, 2 Ld. Raym. 804. Lord Holt says "where a man is obliged to make fences against another, it is enough to say omnes occupatores ought to repair &c., because that lays a charge upon the right of another, which it may be he cannot particularly know."

See *Anonymous case*, 1 Ventr. 264.

But with regard to matters of discharge it is said that even a Corporation cannot prescribe to be discharged of the ancient grand custom, nor yet to receive it, because it is an annual revenue of the Crown, and a casualty as waif and stray, &c.

Further with regard to the king, "no prescription will bind him in a case where he has a right," is said in argument in a case in 38 Ass. f. 227, pl. 22, to which it is replied that prescription runs against the king just as against anybody else, otherwise the lords would lose their franchises by quo warranto.

Upon this point the truth seems to be that strictly at Common Law length of user did not avail against the king[1]. Nullum tempus occurrit regi. Length of enjoyment of a franchise only aggravated the usurpation of the king's prerogative. But this state of things under the circumstances shortly to appear was productive of so much hardship, that after a severe struggle with Edward I. the right of prescribing for franchises against the king was expressly provided by Statute.

It had occurred to certain of the king's counsellors that very few of those who were enjoying franchises would be able to produce their title-deeds for the same, "for that partly by length and process of time, and partly during the troublous times and civill broiles and wars in the raignes of king John

---

[1] 3 Cruise, 2nd edit. p. 506.

and Henry III. many of their charters, records of allowances and other evidences and muniments were destroyed, wasted and made away" (Co. 2 *Inst.* 494), and that as mere length of user gave no right to them, much money might be collected for the royal coffers, by resuming such franchises into the royal hands. Accordingly a proclamation was issued that all who were in enjoyment of franchises should before certain selected persons thereunto appointed show quo jure they held them. This source of revenue was so vigorously worked by the king's officers that "certain it is that there were an exceeding number of writs of quo warranto brought against the prelates and other of the clergy as against the nobles and others of the realme...amongst others a quo warranto was brought against John Warren Earle of Surrey, who appearing before the trustees spake boldly and stoutly against this kinde of proceeding, as our histories doe testifie" (Co. 2 *Inst.* 495). "Quo warranto," said John Warren, "illo warranto," drawing his sword.

So strong was the indignation at these proceedings that by the Statute of Gloucester, 6 Ed. I., their operation was suspended, though the question was not finally decided against the king till later. That Statute recites that "whereas the Realm of England in divers cases, as well upon Liberties as otherwise, wherein the Law failed, to avoid the grievous damages and innumerable disherisons that the default of the Law did bring in, had need of divers helps of new laws and certain new provisions &c., and whereas Prelates, Earls, Barons and other of the realm, that claim to have divers liberties, which to examine and judge the king hath prefixed a day to such, it is provided that the same shall be used after the form of the writ following:"—The writ was a writ to the sheriff of every county commanding him to seize no more franchises, but to permit every man to enjoy them until the king or his justices should next come into the county or until further order. The Statute further provided that all those claiming franchises should come in and prove their rights.

This Statute therefore simply had the operation of an armistice, which lasted for twelve years until the Statutum novum de quo warranto in 18 Ed. I. It appears that in accordance with the earlier Statute the trials upon quo warranto took place before the justices, but they " would not proceed to judgment (the same being final) without being certified de voluntate regis by the writ de libertatibus allocandis, which was not onely a great delay but a great charge to the subject " (Co. 2 *Inst*. 494).

Accordingly by 18 Ed. I. the king granted " that all under his allegiance whatsoever they be, as well spiritual as other, which can verify by good inquest of the Country, or otherwise, that they and their ancestors or predecessors have used any manner of liberties, whereof they were impleaded by the said writs, before the time of King Richard our cousin, or in all his time and have continued hitherto (so that they have not misused such liberties) that the parties shall be adjourned further into a certain day reasonable before the same justices, within the which they may go to our Lord the King with the record of the Justices, signed with their Seal and also the return, and our Lord the King by his letters patents shall confirm their estate." This conceded the whole point and made prescription run against the king.

The remedy for the existing state of things was made complete by the further provision " that all judgments that are to be given in pleas of quo warranto by his Justices at Westminster, after the foresaid Easter, for our Lord the King himself, if the parties grieved will come again before the king, he of his grace shall give them such remedy as before is mentioned."

This was, as Coke remarks, " a speciall grace indeed of the king, that though judgments had been given in any of his Courts at Westminster in pleas of quo warranto for him against any of his subjects (which judgments in law were final against the subjects) yet those judgments notwithstanding the parties grieved should be within the remedy of the Act[1]."

Again, for want of succession the heir cannot be charged

---

[1] The Crown not being mentioned in the 3rd section of the Prescription Act, no right to light can be acquired against the Crown under that section. *Perry v. Eames*, 1891, 1 Ch. 658.

with an annuity not charged upon the land, but merely paid by his ancestors. This appears in 49 E. III. 5.

But, *ibid.*, p. 6, it appears that a prescription will lie for an annuity charged upon a church against the parson, who of course is a continuing body, being a corporation sole.

So it is said that a vill may be bound by prescription to provide a pillory and tumbrel, and that every vill is bound of common right to provide a pair of stocks. As to which quære. 2 Hawk. *Pl. Cr.* 73, c. 11. 3. 2 ; Vin. *Abr.* 262.

CHAPTER IV.

WHAT THINGS MAY BE PRESCRIBED FOR.

So far then as to the persons prescribing, or to be prescribed against.

I shall now say something as to the things of which a prescription can be made. Now I may just here repeat what I began by enunciating, viz. that no prescription can be made of land, and that prescription in the proper sense of the term and the sense in which I am now using it, as distinguished from the larger use, which includes limitation of actions, applies exclusively to incorporeal hereditaments. Markby in his *Elements of Law* treats land as being capable of acquisition by prescription, and declares that Coke so treats it. But Coke does not so treat it: he only refers to § 310, where a prescription can be made of land in an indirect way by prescribing to be tenant in common of land. So that Coke's authority is really the other way. The same is the case with Brooke, *Ab. Pres.* 19: Williams, *Commons*, p. 2, and *Wilkinson v. Proud*, 11 M. and W. 33, is a decision to that effect.

It may be that if one were constructing a logical code there is no reason why the ownership of land should not be capable of being prescribed for just as rights over it less than ownership may. All that I say is that historically in English law the effect of lapse of time upon the ownership of land was provided for by Limitation not Prescription.

It is however worthy of remark that an exception seems to exist as to the soil of the sea-shore, which can apparently be claimed as appurtenant to a manor and by prescription. See Hale, *de Jure maris*, Pt. I. c. IV. VI.; *Constable's Case*, 5 Rep. 106; *King v. Lord Yarborough*, 3 B. and C. 91; Comyns, *Dig. Navigation*, A. B., 1 Sid. 148; 1 Doug. 441.

The reason why no prescription can be made of corporeal hereditaments seems to be explained in *Paramour v. Yardly,* Plowd. 545 a.

The actual case of land is not there mentioned, but it seems to follow from the principle there enunciated. The passage there runs as follows :—

"So a man cannot prescribe to distrain for rent service, or to drive his cattle, for which he has common appendant, out of the land wherein he has common to his own house, for he may do it without prescription," i.e. since he has the right of common it follows that *as incident to that* he has the right to drive them, and therefore does not need to, and therefore cannot, prescribe for such right. So again, *ibid.,* "If a man devises his land to his son and heir in fee simple and dies, the devise is void; for if no such devise had been made the son should have had the land at the same instant that the devise would take effect....if a man devises his land to his son and heirs to have to him and to his heirs of his body, this is a good devise, because it is another estate than he should have had by descent." The common law rule as the devise to the heir in fee simple has now been altered by Section 3 of the Inheritance Act, and the devise takes effect, so that the heir takes as purchaser.

So in the case of land, no prescription can be because there is a better title, viz. the possession.

It was upon this principle that a distinction was attempted to be drawn between a prescription of the *surface* of land and a prescription of the *minerals* lying beneath the surface. The attempt was however ineffectual.

The case was *Wilkinson v. Proud,* 11 M. and W. 33, and it arose in this way. In an action on the case for injury to plaintiff's reversion defendant pleaded that he and his ancestors had actually taken all the coals and veins of coal, &c. time whereof, &c.... It was then argued that no title to land could be claimed by prescription, and that this was a claim of a title to land.

For the defendant it was argued that the mines and minerals under the surface did not lie in livery, since it was impossible to make livery of them, at any rate when they were unopened.

Upon this point Sheppard, Touchstone 96, seems decidedly applicable where it is stated "by the grant of mineras, or fodinas plumbi, &c. or mines of lead, the land itself will pass, if livery of seisin be made thereof; but otherwise it seems not, and then the granter hath by the grant only a power to dig granted to him," i.e. an incorporeal hereditament. And p. 38, Martin *arguendo* cites Mr Preston :—

"A mine may be a corporeal hereditament, for instance if the mine be open and granted, the grant is of a corporeal hereditament. In regard to mines not open at the date of the grant, this distinction (a distinction founded on principle) though no decision is found on the point, may be taken. The grantee has an incorporeal not a corporeal hereditament (*Doe v. Wood*, 2 B. and Ald. 724), an interest which would pass by grant without livery of seisin."

And the case of an unopened mine was asserted to be analogous to the case of a treasure trove which may be claimed by prescription. Co. Litt. 114, 6.

One would have thought, however, with all deference to the authorities thus cited, that the truth was very plainly the other way. The maxim cujus est solum ejus est usque ad cœlum et usque ad inferos clearly avails to make the livery of the surface at any rate a symbolical delivery of the minerals under the surface despite the fact that of course a right merely to take the coals might be given by express grant.

It was held by the Court that this was a claim to land and was bad, but that if the claim had been of a prescriptive right to take coals in the plaintiff's close that would have been a good claim; and the defendant was allowed so to amend upon payment of costs.

But although no claim to land can be made by prescription, there is something like an exception to this in the case of a prescription to be tenant in common of land. Co. Litt. 195 b.

"But joynt tenants cannot be by prescription, because there is a survivor between them, but not between tenants in common." *Ibid.*

A right to enjoy a profit in land in alternis vicibus with other persons may be claimed, *Welden v. Bridgwater*, Cro. El. 421.

With regard even to a claim by prescripton merely to a right to take minerals, it was held in *Hilton v. Earl Granville*, 5 Q. B. 701, that a prescriptive claim by the lord of a manor to work mines *under the copyhold tenements even parcel of the Manor*, without making compensation for any damage caused to any messuages or other buildings by such working, is void as an unreasonable custom.

Now the general rule with regard to prescriptive claims— to be gathered from the cases themselves and stated in Comyns *Dig.* p. 95, is, that every such claim is good *prima facie*, if by possibility it might have had a legal commencement. To this rule there are however exceptions, as will presently appear.

Now Coke 114 a. b lays down with regard to franchises and liberties the rule in the following way :—" As to such franchises and liberties as cannot be seised or forfeited, before the cause of forfeiture appeare of record, no man can make a title by prescription, because that prescription, being but an usage in pais, it cannot extend to such things as cannot be seised nor had without matter of record : as to the goods and chattels of traitors, felons, felons of themselves, fugitives, of those that be put in exigent, deodands, conusance of pleas, to make a corporation, to have a sanctuary to make a coroner, &c. and to make conservators of the peace, &c. But to treasure trove, waifes, estraies, wrecke of sea, to hold pleas, courts of leets, hundreds, &c. infange thiefe, outfange thiefe, to have a parke, warren, royall fishes ; as whales, sturgions, &c. fayres, markets, franke foldage, the keeping of a gaole, tolle, a corporation by prescription and the like a man may make a title by usage and prescription onely without any matter of record."

As to the right to a sanctuary there is an interesting case in the *Year Book*, 1 Hen. VII. 23, from which it is clear that that right cannot be claimed by prescription without charter before the time of memory, and allowance in eyre after the time of memory. One Humphrey Stafford accused of treason for raising an insurrection took refuge in a sanctuary at a place called Culna in Oxfordshire. He was forcibly seized there and taken to the Tower of London. He was brought into the King's Bench on writ of Habeas Corpus. The abbot of Culna claimed him as a refugee in the sanctuary. In support of the privilege he showed it had been exercised from the time of king Edwin, and even brought a charter of king Edwin, "non sigillatam sed cum crucibus signatam." But all the justices were clearly of opinion that the privilege required to be proved by Royal Charter before the time of memory, and by allowance in eyre after the time of memory. The case contains many points of interest, and well repays perusal.

Now although there can be no prescription directly for Catalla felonum et fugitivorum, yet it appears that obliquely they may be prescribed for. A man may claim to have a County Palatine by prescription, and by reason thereof, and as incident thereto, to have bona et catalla proditorum, felonum, etc. Co. Litt. 114 b.

And yet one distinction more it seems should be made. Though a man cannot prescribe to have the goods of a felon, that should apparently be restricted to the goods properly belonging to the felon, and which are forfeited by his conviction,—not to goods of other people which the felon has stolen, and which have been waived; since a man may prescribe to have goods stolen and waived. This comes under the general right of claiming chattels waived, which are none the less in that category because they happen to be in the possession of a felon.

Brooke, *Abr. Estray* 13, puts it thus: "Home ne prescriber in bona fugitivorum et hoc videt' del pper biens del felon, mes home poit prescriber in biens emblees et waives q̂r. felon nad ppertie." And see 46 E. III. 16.

So far as these go therefore they would extend to any goods waived in the possession of a felon whether stolen by him or not, but I think it can only refer to goods stolen *by the felon*, and waived; for if the felon had found some goods that had been stolen by someone else, and waived by their original owner, and by the thief, there seems no reason why they should not become his property. The note in Vin. *Abr.* p. 274 seems to point to this.

In Brooke *Abr.* prescription 64, we find another reason given, or perhaps the same reason really, but stated in a different way. He there states that a man cannot prescribe in catalla felonum or in cognisance of pleas "quar le roy m̄ ne poet ceô av̄ nisi p̄ mattr̄ de record et ideo comen person ne poet este de melior condicion."

But it would appear that there is a distinction, for he states *ibid.* 59, "home poet prescriber tenere pl'ita sed non habere cognic' pli'torum." And as to this see further 9 H. VII. 11.

The reason against prescribing to make a coroner does not seem to be quite the same as that, e.g. as to catalla felonum, because there is no matter of record required here. The rule is however well established. The reason given by Hawkins 2 *Pl. Cr.* 44 c. 9 § 11 is as follows:—"It is clearly supposed by the statute of 28 E. III. 6 that not only the king but also other lords have the franchise of making coroners. From whence it seems reasonable to infer that the king may lawfully claim such franchise by prescription, and that other lords may claim it by grant from the Crown; *but it is a privilege of so high a nature,* that no subject can well entitle himself to it by prescription only."

The same reason would apparently apply to the case of Conservators of the Peace. With regard to them, Hawkins says, 2 *Pl. Cr.* 34, c. 8 § 10, "It is questioned by some whether such power can be claimed by usage, yet if the power of holding pleas and even Courts of record which are of so high a nature and imply a power of keeping the peace within their own precincts may be claimed by usage, as it seems to be certain that they may; it seems strange that the bare authority of keeping the peace in a certain district may not as well be claimed by such usage."

The answer to that would appear to be that Conservators of the Peace were not officers belonging to the justice that a subject could prescribe to administer. They were officers of the king's justice, and although subjects might prescribe for justice of their own, yet no subject could by prescription or otherwise claim to administer the king's justice, and hence could not claim by prescription to appoint officers of that justice. The whole history of the rise of the Courts of Justice as they now exist is most interesting, being as it is a history of the rivalry existing between the popular courts and their justice, and the king's Courts and their justice, which ultimately, as being the more powerful, prevailed, so that the 'King's Peace' was well kept over all the realm. This lies aside from the line of my inquiry, but it arises incidentally in this question of the Conservators of the Peace. In a case in 21 E. IV. 67 of trespass against a mayor for committing a man to prison the mayor justified because it had been used time out of mind that the mayors have been Conservators of the Peace and have used for affrays done in their presence to commit the offenders to prison till they have found surety of the peace. Brian said "you have no such power but to commit him to prison till he has made fine, and the power cannot rest upon the usage," quod Pigott concessit.

That a man may prescribe to hold Courts of his own, and so administer justice, appears clear from the passage of Coke cited above where prescription to hold pleas, to have a Court Leet, or Hundred, to have Infangthief, and Outfangthief is stated to be good.

As regards a Court Leet this seems rather inconsistent with the account given by Blackstone, 4 *Commen.* 273 stating that the Court Leet is a King's Court. His account is as follows :

"The Court Leet or view of frankpledge is a Court of record held once in the year and not oftener, within a particular hundred, lordship or Manor before the Steward of the leet, *being the king's Court granted* by Charter to the Lords of those hundreds or Manors. Its original intent was to view the frankpledges, that is the freemen within the liberty; who we may remember according to the institution of the Great Alfred were all mutually pledges for the good behaviour of each other. Besides this, the preservation of the peace and the chastisement of divers minute offences against the public good are the objects both of the Court leet and the sheriff's tourn; which have exactly the same jurisdiction, one being only a larger species of the other, extending over more territory but not over more causes."

Now it is quite true that the Court leet was a King's Court, a criminal Court. But owing to the fact that it was a Court the right to hold which was granted to subjects, as soon as there began to be any competition between royal justice and private justice, the Court leet, though originally having a jurisdiction derived from the king, took its place in the struggle on the side of popular justice.

If this be borne in mind no difficulty arises in the account of Blackstone or in the following case. 21 H. VII. 40.

"And also in a leet a man may prescribe to have of every man that makes an affray or bloodshed a certain sum of money; and that is good: and he may prescribe to distrain for it, and to sell the distress *since this is the Court of the King* and he derives his interest from the king." See also Br. *Abr. Pres.* pl. 40. But this *prescription* of private justice would appear to have been subject to a very important limitation, as appears from the case of *Pill v. Towers*, Cro. E. 791.

There the defendant "made a conusance as bailiff to Sir Fulk Grevil for the amercement of a free tenant within his Manors; and shews that Sir F. Grevil was seised in fee of the Manor of D. and that he and all those whose estate, &c. have had a *Court baron* within the Manor before his Steward of the Manor, tenendum from 3 weeks to 3 weeks; and alledgeth a custom to have suit of court from all his free tenants of the manor; and that if any of them made default, and his default was presented by the homage they had used there to amerce him and the amercement to affeer, and the lord had used to distrain such a tenant for such an amercement, per aliqua bona vel catalla sua within the Manor; and for an amercement for this cause the distress was taken, &c." The plaintiff demurs and it was resolved by the whole Court that the avowry was insufficient.

"First because he prescribes to have a Court baron within his manor, whereas it is of common right and cannot be by prescription for it is incident to a Manor, for Walmsley said *usage is not but where there is a defect of Common right;* but here it stands with Common right and therefore is not good." The defendant then said that it was good by custom in aid of prescription: but the Court shewed that it is not good as a custom.

"Whereas it is said that it shall be maintained by custom, in regard the prescription is to hold it before the Steward of the Manor *which is against Common right* (for of common right it ought to be holden before the suitors) yet it is not good; for a Court baron cannot be holden but before the suitors, and sometimes before the bailiff and suitors as by writ: and by plaint it shall be before the suitors only; *but in no case without the suitors; and one cannot have a Court by prescription but where he cannot have it otherwise.*"

And all the justices agreed with him that he could not have a Court Baron by prescription; *but he may by prescription enlarge the authority thereof as to hold pleas above* 40s. *and the like.*

There is one case which would seem to show that just as a man may prescribe to administer justice, so he may claim to have it administered to him in a particular Court only. Thus in the *Year Book* 2 E. IV. 18 there is a case where a man was impleaded of trespass and battery, and he pleaded that the place where the assault took place was within the precinct of the Monastery of Westminster, and that all places within the said precinct were privileged places, and a sanctuary for all debts, trespasses, felonies, and treasons; and that all actions of debt and trespass within the said precinct had, from time whereof, &c., been impleaded before the Commissioners and demanded judgment.

The judges agreed that the prescription was bad as being against common right, but held that with ancient charter and usage it might have stood. But Laicon goes on to say, "if a man be impleaded of land in London he may say that time out of mind lands in London have been impleaded in the hustings before the Mayor," quod Danby concessit; and further said that the same held good of the Cinque Ports; and Needham added that it did also in Chester and Wales.

The justices in *Pill v. Towers* afterwards went on to show that the claim to distrain was bad, because it was a claim to distrain the goods of the offender in any part of the manor, which would mean a claim to distrain on the lands of one who did not offend. On this point, however, some of the justices differed, and thought it might be good. But in this particular case they all agreed that the acts done did not come within the prescription made; since here the distress had been made of the beasts of the under-tenant, while the prescription made was merely to distrain on the offender. But the claim was not bad on the ground of its being a prescription to distrain on his own land, for that is good. Br. *Abr. Pres.* pl. 1. The reason for which is given in a case in the *Year Book*, 6 H. VIII. 5. That was a case of distress, and the defendant prescribed to distrain on his own land: it was held good, for it was the beasts of the plaintiff that were subject to the distress, and not the land made chargeable.

From the case of *Pill and Towers, sup.* then it appears how the prescription for a Court is limited. From that case it appears that no Court can be prescribed for against common right; nor a Court that is a matter of common right; and that prescription is only allowed in aid of other means, and only when the Court being established cannot be justified on any other ground. The nature of the Court Baron and Customary Court of Copyholders appears from Coke 58 a. As to the place of sitting he says: "The Court Baron must be holden on some part of that which is within the Manor, for if it be holden out of the Manor it is voyd: unless a lord being seised of two or three manors hath usually time out of minde kept at one of his Manors Courts for all the said Manors, then by custome such Courts are sufficient in Law, albeit they be not holden within the severall mannors." Even in a private Court properly established it would appear that no prescription will lie to give any jurisdiction properly belonging to the king alone. Thus a man cannot prescribe to levy Fines in his Court, of lands within his Manor. For Fine is a record which no man can have by prescription, being a prerogative of the Crown, and the king upon every Concord is donor, which a man can't be by prescription. Vin. *Abr.* 275. Glanvil 7, c. 1. But in *Countess Dowager of Pembroke v. Earl of Burlington*, Hardres 423, it was held upon demurrer by Hale, C. B., "that return of writs may be claimed by prescription as appertaining to a manor." And so it appears in quo warranto in 42 Eliz., where the law is admitted to be so, though the prescription was not well laid there to entitle the party to it. And more especially may it be claimed as appertaining to an Honour, as was held in 19 Jac. in Howard's case, in the case of the Honour of Chur. "For Honours have more large incidents than Manors have."

It must be noticed that where a thing may be prescribed for, all the usual incidents of that thing follow, and such usual incidents cannot therefore be prescribed for. Sometimes un-usual incidents may be gained by prescription, as appeared in the case of the Court Baron above. But it is not every un-usual incident that may be thus gained. This principle is well illustrated by the Case of a Corporation. Thus "A body politick, as it is called by Littleton, is also called a corporation or a body incorporate...And this body politick or incorporate may commence and be established three manner of ways, viz. by prescription, by letters patent, or by Act of Parliament." Co. Litt. 350 a.

But though a corporation may be established by pre-scription, it cannot by prescription gain a right to make another corporation. Co. Litt. 114 b. So too Br. *Abr. Customs* pl. 40.

The citizens of London prescribed in usage that a guild or fraternity may make another guild and fraternity; but the custom was condemned, for none may do it but the king or he who has the king's Charter to do it by express words. See too 49 Ass. 8, p. 321.

It seems that the Chief Justice of the Common Bench has by prescription the right to appoint to the office of exigenter. And that appointment to the office by the queen, even made during a vacancy in the Chief Justiceship, is null and void against an appointment made by the Chief Justice as soon as he is appointed. *Skrogges v. Coleshil.* Dyer, 175 b.

It will by now appear fairly clear what franchises cannot be claimed by prescription, and why not. Among the most im-portant of the franchises which are not in need of matter of record, and can therefore be prescribed for, is the franchise of a forest. This is a right which was of great importance in early days.

A forest is defined by Manwood, *Forest Law*, cap. 1, section 1, as follows :—"A forest is a certain territory of woody grounds and fruitful pastures privileged for wild beasts and fowls of forest, chase and warren, to rest and abide in, in the safe protection of the King, for his princely delight and pleasure; which territory of ground so privileged is meered and bounded with unremovable markes, meeres and boundaries, either known by matter of record, or else by prescription, and also replenished with wild beasts of venery or chase, and with great coverts of vert, for the succour of the said wild beasts to have their abode in. For the preservation and continuance of which said place, together with the vert and venison, there are certain particular laws, privileges and offices belonging to the same, meet for that purpose, that are only proper unto a forest, and not to any other place. Therefore a Forest doth chiefly consist of these four things, that is to say of vert, venison, particular laws and privileges, and of certain meet officers appointed for that purpose, to the end that the same may the better be preserved and kept for a place of recreation and pastime meet for the royal dignity of a Prince."

It is to be observed that the forest is a privilege, and not as the word is now generally used, the tract of country. The lands within the forest might perfectly well belong to other persons. This appears from Manwood, ch. 10, section 1 : "Much more if by the laws of this realm Kings and Princes may pull down houses and churches that are already builded to make forests in such places where they please to have forests, they may by the same laws restrain and forbid all inhabitants and *all those that have lands or woods* within forests to erect or build any more houses or buildings than are already builded there without especial license of the King or his justice in eyre."

And in the Charta de Foresta 9 Hen. III. which contained many provisions for the regulation of forests we find cap. 11, 12 provisions how a freeman may use his own land in a forest.

Everyone remembers how continual were the outcries against the Norman kings by reason of these forest rights. By that same Charter de Foresta a very considerable concession was wrung from Henry III. All lands of other people afforested by Hen. II., Richard or John were to be disafforested.

An account of the forest laws is to be found in Manwood. They are very severe.

The laws were enforced by various courts peculiar to the forest. The Woodmote, or forty-day Court, was held before the verderers every forty days. It was merely a court of enquiry as to offences. The Court of Swainmote was also held before the verderers three times a year. All freeholders within the forest and the reeve and four men of every vill within the forest were bound to attend. The Court of Justice Seat was held once every three years. It punished all offences against, and decided all claims under the forest laws; subject to appeal to the King's Bench. Co. 4 *Inst.* 295, 297, " But what if the justice in eyre give an erroneous judgment ? what remedy hath the party gained ? He may have a writ of error out of the chancery returnable unto the King's Bench and then justice shall be done."

It appears that originally the chief justice in eyre of the forest was created by writ like the other justices in eyre. But by 27 Hen. VIII. c. 24 it is provided that he is to be appointed by letters patent.

In Sir William Jones's Reports, p. 266, appear " Notes taken at a Justice Seate for the Forrest of Wyndsor in the County of Berks; London, the 24th day of September, 1632, at Wyndsor." And a great many cases are there reported as having been decided.

Not only the lands within the forest, but certain lands in the purlieus of the forest, were subject to special regulations. But those in the latter case were of a modified description. (See Manwood, ch. 20, 86.)

All these matters with regard to forests are now matters of ancient history. From the Charta de Foresta the forest rights were looked upon as a grievance and limited. By 16 Car. I. c. 16 Commissioners were appointed to ascertain the bounds of the forests, and any place in England or Wales where no Court of Justice Seat, Swainmote or Woodmote had been held, or no verderers had been chosen or regard made for 60 years before the first year of Charles I. was to be absolutely freed from all forest laws.

It does not appear to be absolutely certain that a forest could be prescribed for. Coke does not mention it among the franchises that can be so acquired, though he does mention the smaller rights of park and warren, which were included in the greater right of a forest. And it is easy to see that a claim to a forest was not one that was likely to be often brought to issue. But that is no reason why it should not be a right capable of being gained by prescription, at any rate with allowance in eyre. Questions of prescription for a forest may well have been infrequent for another reason. Such a claim might generally be held to be nothing but a claim to a chase. For unless the grant of the forest contained also a grant of the right to the forest courts expressly, the grant would be held only to pass a chase. As Coke says 4 *Inst.* p. 313, " The king being seised of a forest, did grant the forest to another in fee, the grantee shall have no forest because he hath no power to make justices of forest, to hold courts, &c.; but yet though it cannot take effect ex vi termini as a forest, yet together with the game the same shall pass as a free chase for the savages.... For as hath been said every forest is a free chase et quiddam amplius."

But that the full right of a forest could be granted appears from Coke, 4 *Inst.* p. 314, " But if the king doth grant a forest to a subject and granteth further that, upon requests made in the Chancery, he and his heirs shall have justices of the forest, then the subject hath a forest in law."

Of course a prescription to a forest itself would not be touched by the Charta de Foresta, as were prescriptions of other rights within a forest. Thus in the case of the inhabitants of Egham alluded to before in considering who might prescribe (Sir W. Jones, 275), Mr Attorney said that prescription to cut down wood was not good, for there can be no prescription since the Statute of Charta de Foresta, c. 4, which is that all was to be done after that time without the king's license should be punishable. He also said that a claim to fell wood per visum forrestariorum vel verdariorum was not good. It should have been by view and allowance of the verderers.

And a case was cited in 6 Jac. to the effect that in a chase a man might prescribe to fell wood, *because a chase was not within the Charta de Foresta.* And this seems to have been allowed.

Now it has been seen that where there was a grant of a forest without grant of the right to the forest courts, that was merely a grant of a chase. As to matters of record in connexion with forests, and whether they be forests in law or only in name, see Coke, 4 *Inst.* 298—the case of the forests of Bowland and Leicester.

The record in the case of a forest differs from the record in the case of felon's goods, because it is merely an incident of the thing itself when gained, and not an incident of the title to the thing. It is not the record that makes the forest, but the forest that makes the record. In the case of the felon's goods it is the record that makes them claimable by anyone but the felon himself.

Now a chase gave a right of sport without the severe forest laws for its protection. Thus the owners of lands within a chase were not restricted in the use of them in the same way that those owning lands within a forest were. In the case of the forest of Bowland cited above, the judges further resolved " that if they be but free chases and no forests in law that then the owners of woods within such chases may cut down timber or wood growing therein without view of any officer or license of any." But this was not an absolute right as in lands freed from a chase ; it must be so exercised as not to interfere with the enjoyment of the chase. The difference was that in a chase he could do it without license, in a forest he might either prescribe to do it, but that with view and allowance of the verderers, or " if he hath no such prescription the law doth appoint him a means to fell both wood and timber, so it be no prejudice to the game, but sufficient is left besides, and that is by a writ of ad quod damnum upon return whereof the king doth license him." Coke, 4 *Inst.* p. 298, Fitzherbert, *Nat. brev.* 226 f.

A park is a right less extensive than a chase. It is less extensive rather in point of size than in point of right.

A park is an enclosed chase. It extends only over a person's own grounds. It therefore falls as far short of a chase as

7—2

a chase does of a forest. It is more like a reservation to a man of the rights he would naturally have on his own land than a grant of any new right. To a park three things are necessary, 11 Rep. 87 b, Cro. Car. 60. (1) A grant from the crown or prescription based on such grant. (2) Enclosure by pale, wall or hedge. (3) Beasts of park. Cruise, *Dig.* p. 248, vol. 3. Where all the deer are destroyed it is no more accounted a park : " for a park consists of vert, venison and enclosure, and if it be determined in any of these it is a total disparking."

A warren is the next of the sporting franchises I shall have to consider. But the ordinary right of sporting, not the franchise, which is of course a right that may be gained by prescription, may be conveniently treated in conjunction with these franchises. It has given rise to an interesting controversy.

A free warren is a franchise to have and keep certain wild beasts and fowls called game within some inclosed space. Its true character will be best apprehended by bearing in mind that it is parcel of the largest right of all, the right of forest. Where it is granted within a forest, chase or park it is a deduction from that right, and gives a right to exclude the owner of such larger right, which a mere right of sporting would not. It is laid down in the *case of Monopolies*, 11 Rep. 87 b, that none can make a park, chase or warren without the king's license : for that is quodammodo to appropriate those creatures which are ferae naturae and nullius in bonis to himself, and to restrain them of their natural liberty.

The granting of free warren was, according to Spelman (gloss. s.v. Warrenna) introduced into England by the Normans. In the Charter of foundation of Battle Abbey (Dugd. *Mon.* Vol. I. 317) is found a grant of free warren : and there is no doubt that the right was frequently granted by the Normans and Plantagenets (Cruise, *Dig.* 3, 249, Black. 2 *Comm.* 417). These grants of free warren have caused Blackstone (*ib.*) to conclude that upon the introduction of the Feudal System into England as modified by the gemote of Salisbury the sole right to kill all game became vested in the king. But the original right of killing game upon his own land vested in each man ratione soli was no more taken out of him—than were the other rights appertaining to the ownership of the soil upon his becoming a tenant in capite. And the grants of free warren were, as pointed out above, not mere rights of killing game.   The acts requiring a qualification of property to enable a man to kill game upon his own property are not acts which make a grant of the right to those having the qualification, but they take away the right from those who had not that qualification : which does not seem more unjust, as Cruise declares, than not to grant to those having lands, but below the required amount.   The reason of these statutes appears clear from the preamble to the first of them, 13 Ric. II. c. 13, " divers artificers, labourers, servants and grooms keep greyhounds and dogs, and on the holy days when good Christian people be at Church hearing divine service, they go a hunting in parks and warrens and conigrees of lords and others, to the very great destruction of the same, and sometimes under such colour they make their assemblies, conferences and conspiracies for to rise and disobey their allegiance ; it is therefore ordained that no artificer, labourer or other layman which hath not lands or tenniments to the value of 40s. by the year, nor any priest to the value of £10 shall keep any dogs, nets or engines to destroy deer, hares nor conies, nor other gentlemen's game upon pain of one year's imprisonment." And the statutes 1 Jac. I. c. 27, 7 Jac. I. c. 11, 22 and 23 Car. II. c. 25 quoted by Blackstone as giving the right to persons qualified as therein mentioned, only do so after a prior prohibition of everybody.   They therefore make directly against the proposition in support of which they are quoted, since there would not have been any need of prohibiting a right which was not possessed.   And I think that without going further into it the question is quite plain from a case in the *Year Book*, 12 H. VIII. 10, when it was held that if a man drive a stag out of a forest and kill him he gains no property in the stag : but if the stag comes of himself beyond the limits of the forest then anyone, qualified to kill, may kill and take him, since stags are ferae naturae et nullius in bonis, and the maxim capiat qui capere potest applies.

Now it appears that just as the king could not create a forest or chase over another man's land without his consent,

Co. 4 *Inst.* 401, so he could not grant a right of free warren on any lands other than those of the grantee himself. Now this right of free warren could be claimed by prescription as belonging to his own lands: but as will be seen later on it could not by prescription be gained over the land of another. Though by other means it might come to be enjoyed over the land of another, in this way:—The grant might be to a man in respect of his own lands. This right might then be granted to another. Hence it could lawfully be created so as to come to take effect over the land of another. Now these rights of park, chase and warren are not rights included in the owner-ship of the soil, and are not extinguished by merger: for the essence of them is that they must be created over a man's own land. Coke, 4 *Inst.* 318, says that they are collateral in-heritances, and not issuing out of the soil as common does: so that if one has a chase over the land of another and purchases the land, the chase remains. From this it follows that where there is land subject to a warren, if it is intended to pass the warren upon a grant of the land, the warren must be specially granted, or specially reserved. For if the land be merely granted without more, the warren does not pass, nor does it remain unless reserved since the land is granted discharged of all things. Bro. *Abr. Warr.* 3 Dyer, 30 b. pl. 209. See a case of prescription of warren over a manor *R. v. Talbot,* Cro. Car. 311.

In a prescription of warren within a forest there must have been an allowance of it in eyre, otherwise it was not good. *Harrison's Case,* Sir W. Jones, p. 267.

Of course where there exists a right of warren over a man's land that excludes his right of sporting ratione soli.

The importance of the difference between the right of warren and the mere right of sporting has come out well in the discussions that have taken place upon Inclosure Acts, where waste lands of a manor have been inclosed. Such an act, unlike a grant which cannot be derogated from, does not take away from the lord anything but what is expressly mentioned. Hence, if there be a right of warren in the lands, that remains to the lord and he has the right of sporting. But if there were no right of warren, but merely the right of sporting, that being one of the ordinary incidents of the land, goes with the land, and the other lord thenceforth has no right. (*Robinson v. Wray*, L. R. 1 C. P. 490 ; *Lord Leconfield v. Dixon*, L. R. 3 Exch. 30 ; *Ewart v. Graham*, 7 H. L. Cas. 331 ; *Sowerby v. Smith*, L. R. 8 C. P. 514, 9 C. P. 524.) Of course since 1 and 2 Will. IV. c. 32, which abolished the qualification required to kill game, the ordinary right of sporting is a right that may be prescribed for just as any other incorporeal hereditament.

Closely analogous to the free warren was the free fishery[1]. The subject of fisheries is by no means so clear as it might be. A free fishery appears to have been a right of fishing in a public river. It seems to have been claimed as a royal prerogative, with quite as little justification as the afforesting of land other than the king's demesnes, and by Magna Charta this usurpation was put an end to by the provision that where the banks had first been defended in the time of King John they should be laid open. The number was further reduced by the Charters of Henry III. by including all those fenced in the time of Richard I.; so that any claim to a free fishery must absolutely be proved irrespective of prescription, up to the time of legal memory; and no prescription save that from the time of legal memory will do. The question of the nature of the three rights of free fishery, several fishery, and common fishery, is discussed and a great many authorities cited in Co. Litt. 122 note.

The case of *Weld v. Hornby*, 7 East, 195, was an important one in connexion with fishery in public rivers. It was there held that the erection of weirs across public rivers was a public nuisance, according to Magna Charta, which had forbidden the erection of new ones, or the enlarging of those then existing,— and that therefore the stells erected in the river Eden by Lord Lonsdale and the Corporation of Carlisle, were illegal. And that though acquiescence might bind those whose private interests merely were affected yet that no acquiescence could bind the public to submit to the nuisance.

---

[1] See Brown *on Limitation*, pp. 154—202, where the subject is gone into at great length.

Among the franchises enumerated by Coke as claimable by prescription without record are fairs or markets. Now it was usual at the time of the grant of the patent by the king for the holding of a fair or market to execute at the same time a writ of ad quod damnum, that it may be found whether the grant will be to the damage of neighbouring markets. If it is so found the patent will not be granted; and even if the writ is answered by finding that there is no damnum, that is not conclusive. For in *Sir Oliver Butler's Case*, 2 Vent. 344, the Lord Chancellor Finch held that the return was not conclusive and that where a patent could be proved at any time to have been granted to the prejudice of a subject the king was to allow him to use his name in a scire facias.

Thus Fitzherbert, *N. B.* 184, in a note commenting on the case of W. de Clynton in 13 E. III. states that if the market were to be held in the adjoining vill on the same day as an existing market that should be intended a nuisance. But if the market were held on a different day it should be put in issue, in a scire facias by the king to repeal the patent, whether it was a nuisance or not, see 11 H. IV. 55. A fortiori was a market erected without patent, a nuisance if held on the same day as one in the next vill; and though held on a different day, if so found by a jury in an action on the case for nuisance. *Yard v. Ford*, 2 Saund. 172. An action on the case for a nuisance for disturbance of a market laboured under this special disability incident to its nature. It was a possessory action and therefore considered by the Courts as in the nature of an eject-ment. Hence if the plaintiff had lain by for 20 years or more and allowed a market to be held in the next vill on the same day as his own, the uninterrupted possession was considered an absolute bar to the action. *Holcroft v. Herl*, 1 Bos. and Pul. 400.

The grant of a market did not of itself give a right to the grantee to exclude persons having private shops within the limits of the franchise, from selling marketable commodities on market days. *Mayor of Macclesfield v. Chapman*, 12 M. and W. 18.

But such right might be annexed by prescription to a

market as an additional incident. *Mosley v. Walker*, 7 B. and C. 40.

But a grant of a market did carry with it some important incidents. Thus the grant implied a grant of a court of Record, the *Court of Piepoudre*, to try disputes arising in the market. See Coke, 2 *Inst.* 220. 3 Reeves, CXX. p. 293.

Tolls were frequently granted with markets but were not necessarily incident thereto.

Treasure trove was another franchise that might be prescribed for. Treasure trove did not, as in Roman Law, belong half to the finder and half to the owner of the land, but it belonged to the king—"Quod non capit Christus capit fiscus" —unless granted away or prescribed for in some other. "Treasure trove is when any gold or silver in coin, plate or bullyon hath been of ancient time hidden, wheresoever it be found, whereof no person can prove any property, it doth belong to the King or to some Lord or other by the King's grant or prescription." Gold and silver in mines is not treasure trove, that belongs to the King for another reason. "It is to be observed that veyns of gold and silver in the grounds of subjects belong to the king by his prerogative." Co. 3 *Inst.* 132. There seems no reason why mines of gold, &c. should not have been equally capable of prescription. But one would imagine that either right concerned a matter of so infrequent occurrence as to make proof of its exercise extremely difficult.

The concealment of treasure trove was according to the older authorities punishable by death or loss of member. Bract. li. 3. fo. 120. Fleta, lib. 4. ca. 19. Glanvil, li. 1. ca. 1. li. 14. ca. 2. But later it was resolved that it was punishable only by fine and imprisonment, 22 Ass. 99, 2 Hawk. *P. C.* 67.

It was the duty of the finder to report it to the Coroner. (Stat. de officio coronatoris, 4 E. I.)

The distinction between franchises that can, and those that cannot be prescribed for, appears perhaps nowhere more plainly than in the case of waifs. Waifs are goods stolen and left by the felon on being pursued for fear of apprehension. They are not the felon's own goods which require either the record of conviction where he has been captured; or where a hue and cry has been raised and the felon has fled, until found of record that he fled for the felony. 3 Hawk. *P. C.* 450.

When the felon has fled and left the goods, the sheriff or the bailiff of the prison having the franchise of waifs may seize them. And unless the owner makes pursuit of the felon and gets him convicted of the robbery within a year and a day, the goods then belong to the owner of the franchise. See *Foxley's Case*, 5 Rep. 109. Waifs are only such stolen goods as the felon had in his possession *at the time* he fled, and not goods that he had previously stolen and hidden, intending to fetch them at a future time. Brooke, *Abr. Estrays*, 9, 29 E. III. 29.

Estrays are tame beasts that stray into a manor. The owner of the franchise of estrays can, by seizing such beast and proclaiming it at the two next market towns on two market days, at the end of a year and a day acquire a property therein good against everybody including persons under disability. *Constable's Case*, 5 Rep. 108 b. If the owner claims the animal within the year and a day, he can have it back on payment of the cost of keep. 1 Roll. ab. 879. The estray may not be used in any way during the year and a day, save of necessity, *e.g.*, milking a cow. See *Bagshawe v. Goward*, Cro. Jac. 148.

The next franchise that I shall consider is that of wreck. The subject is discussed at length in *Constable's Case*, 5 Rep. 105 b. It appears that wreck consists of such goods as are cast on shore after a ship has been lost, provided that no man or other living creature escape so that the owner may be known, as was declared by Stat. West. I. 3 Ed. I., c. 4, in affirmance of the Common Law. "Where a man, a dog or a cat escape quick out of the ship it is not to be wreck." Wreck is only prescribable for when it has come to shore, for while it is flotsam, jetsam or ligan, it belongs to the king. It appears that between high and low water mark, the Common Law and the Admiral have divisum imperium—the Common Law when the tide is down, the Admiral when the tide is high.

Now there seems to be no doubt that whales and sturgeons and such like are Royal fish, and that they may be prescribed for. Co. Litt. 114 b: 39 E. III. 35. But it is preferable to consider the question of prescription of Royal animals in the case of swans, which are of so superior and ethereal a nature as to have caused Coke in the report of a case of the *Queen v. Lady Joan Young*, 7 Rep. 15 b. to burst forth into an eulogium and to quote the Latin poet in praise.   He says, "The cock swan is an emblem or representation of an affectionate and true husband to his wife, above all other fowls; for the cock swan holdeth himself to one female only, and for this cause nature hath conferred on him a gift beyond all others; that is to die so joyfully that he sings sweetly when he dies; upon which the poet saith—

> 'Dulcia defecta modulatur carmina lingua
> Cantator Cygnus funeris ipse sui.' "

Now with regard to swans there are many curious questions. Thus, it makes a difference whether the swan in question is a white swan or no, and if so, whether marked or not, and if marked, whether marked by a person having a right to use a mark.   For it appears from a Statute passed in the 22nd year of Edward the Fourth, c. 6, that this right was restricted.   It was provided "that no person of what estate, degree or condition he be (other than the son of our Sovereign Lord the King) from the feast of Saint Michael next coming, shall have or possess any such mark or game of his own, or any other to his use shall have or possess any such game or mark, except he have lands or tenements of the estate of freehold to the yearly value of five marks above all yearly charges."   It was agreed in an action of trespass brought by Lord Strange and Sir John Charlton, jointly, against three defendants, that none has any right to a swan mark unless he has lands worth five marks a year clear; and then only by grant of the king or his officers authorised thereto, or by *prescription*.   And a swan mark when thus enjoyed may be granted over, a precedent of which in the time of Henry VI. is given by Coke as having been seen by him[1].

---

[1] "Notum sit omnib' hominib' praesentib' et futuris, quod ego J. Steward, miles, dedi et concessi Tho' fil' meo primogenito et haeredibus suis cigni- not' meam armor' meor', prout in margine laterali pingitur, quae mihi jure hereditar' descendeb' post mort' J. Steward mil' patris mei: habend' sibi

In the case of Lord Strange and Sir J. Charlton it appeared that Lord Strange owned a cock swan and Sir J. Charlton the hen, and the mutual faith of the couple apparently was considered a reason for applying the maxim "pater est quem nuptiae demonstrant," and holding that the cygnets belonged to them equally in common.

There was an ancient officer called magister deductus cygnorum who certainly continued until the time of James I., whose duty it was to collect for the king swans strayed. In a case in the *Year Book*, 7 Hen. VI. 27 b., these four points were decided:—

1. That every one that has swans within the private waters in his manor has property in them.

2. That a game of swans within a manor may be prescribed for as well as a warren or park.

3. That a person having such a game of swans may prescribe for them to swim on the waters of another.

4. That a swan may be an estray.

Now with regard to the claim by prescription to have swans and other things in the same way, care had to be taken how the claim was alleged. In the case of the *Queen v. Lady Joan Young* the prescription was held bad, because the plea was to have all wild swans, and not marked, and "nidificant, gignent et frequentant" within the manor. This was too wide. Just as it would be too wide in a prescription for a warren to say all pheasants and partridges, nidificantes, &c. within the manor. The claim should be to have free warren of them within the manor. "For although they are nidificantes, &c. within the manor, he cannot have them jure privilegii but

---

et heredibus suis, una cum omnibus cygnis et cygniculis cum dicta nota baculi nodati signat' (and a ragged staff was painted in the margin), sub condicione, quod quilib' feria solis durante vita a gula Augusti usque ad Carniprivium apud domum meam de Darford, unum cignicil' bene signat' mihi aut meis deliberet, quod si defecerit tunc volo quod hoc praesens chirographum cassetur penitus et pro nihilo habeatur. In Cuj' rei testimon' ad instant' Matildae uxor' meae, meum sigill' secretum Christi Crucifixi praesentib' feci apponi. Hiis testibus R. Clerico, J. D. Conyers, Alano Fabro, et al' dat' apud dom' meam mansional' de Darf' in vigilia S. Dunst' ep' an' regni Regis Hen. post conquest' Angliae Sexti 14."

so long as they are within the place." 7 Rep. 18 a. Now though swans are Royal birds yet they may be prescribed for, since such claim might have a legal origin in grant from the Crown. Instances of such grant are to be found in *Rot. Parl.* 30 Ed. III. part 2. 20, where the king granted to C. W. all wild swans unmarked between Oxford and London for seven years.

In *Rot. Parl.* 16 R. II. p. 1. num. 39 is a grant of all wild swans unmarked in the county of Cambridge, to B. Bereford, Knight.

Frankfoldage (libera falda) which Coke, Litt. 114 b. holds a good subject of prescription was held to be good in 8 Rep. 125, where one Jeffery at Hay brought trespass against William at Ford, and Robert Gray for breaking his fold at Hastings. See *Punsary v. Leader*, Le. 11 pl. 25 and 26 Eliz., and *John de Ledgeford's Case*, 2 Brownl. 287 : and 3 E. III. 3 a.

Another kind of right with regard to the folding of sheep was prescribed for in the *Year Book* of 5 H. VII. 9. There in defence to trespass for taking sheep the defendant said, that the land where the trespass was alleged was his free tenement, and that he and those whose estate he had had used time, &c. that if any depasture his sheep with the sheep of the defendant by day, to have them in the night for the dung. By reason whereof he took them at night and released them in the morning. This was held a good prescription. For not only may it have lawful beginning, but the plaintiff has quid pro quo, the pasture for the dung.

So in *Thornell v. Lassels*, Cro. J. 27 Pasch. 2 Jac., it was held a reasonable prescription to have pasturage for two horses in a meadow of 1000 acres till the grass is mowed, " for being in so great a quantity of land cannot defoul or debruise the grass so, but that the hay may well be made thereof." *Dickins v. Hampstead*, Gibb. 87 Trin. 2 and 3 Geo. II., is authority for saying that a prescription to have all the loppings of all trees called pollards in a certain place is good.

A strong illustration of how completely all the profits of land, as distinguished from the land itself, may be prescribed for is afforded by the case of rent. It seems that the rent of land may be prescribed for, 13 Ass. 4. The case of claims to toll has given rise to a good deal of discussion.

There are two kinds of toll, 2 Roll. *Abr. Toll*, 522: Br. *Abr. Toll*, pl. 6; Toll Thorough, a toll for passing over a highway; and Toll Traverse, a toll for passing over the land of a private person. It has been laid down that toll traverse can be prescribed for, but not toll thorough. Thus Fitzherbert, *Nat. brev.* 518 a, Hale's Edition, p. 227, "Toll traverse lies in prescription, but not toll thorough, for it is an oppression of the people." See 22 Ass. 58. It is also said, 20 E. III., Fitzh. *N. B., ibid.,* that toll traverse may be by prescription or grant: but toll thorough cannot be by prescription or grant. The true account, so far as it can be collected, seems to be as follows: Every prescription being in theory founded upon a grant, imports consideration of some kind. Now for toll traverse the consideration is plain; since the right of passing over land where one had not before any right is in itself the consideration. But with regard to toll thorough the case is different. For as laid down in *Smith v. Shepherd*, Cro. E. 710, "the inheritance of every man in the king's highway is prior to all prescriptions." That apparently means, that unless the person claiming the toll can show that he and his ancestors were seised of the soil of the highway before the public had a right of passing over it, the contest is between two rights, both resting entirely on length of user; that of the public to pass, and that of the claimant to demand his tolls, and the claim of the individual must therefore fail. Another reason is that such a prescription would be bad on the ground that it could not have had a legal commencement. *Prideaux v. Ward*, 2 Lev. 96. For unless the claimant does some service to the public by way of consideration, as *e.g.* repairing the highway or bridges, the king even is unable to grant the toll to the oppression of the people. See *Lord Pelham v. Pickersgill*, 1 T. R. at p. 669. Of course if the claimant can show seisin before the public had a right of way, the grant of the soil to the public for a highway would be a sufficient consideration. For if a person who dedicates his land to the public for particular purposes only, is allowed to demand a toll, a fortiori

should he who dedicates it for all purposes. This appears plain
from the case of *Mayor &c. of Yarmouth v. Eaton*, 3 Burr. 1402,
where the question being whether the Corporation could claim
port duties without setting forth the consideration on which
the prescription was founded, Lord Mansfield said, " the making
a port is itself a consideration, it may never require repair;
therefore I do not know that it is necessary to show repair."

Lord Pelham v. Pickersgill, ubi sup. was a case where the
land had been private property before the public gained a
highway. It was found as a fact in that case that William the
Conqueror was seised of the Manor of Bure and the ground
and soil thereof, and it continued in the Crown till the reign
of Charles I., by whom the tolls were severed from the manor.

" Therefore in the present case," says Ashurst, " toll thorough
and toll traverse are the same thing. The only reason why
a distinction is in general taken between them is, because in
the former it cannot be shown that the road was originally the
soil of a private person. Where there was an ancient highway
the king could not grant a toll thorough unless something
were to be performed for the benefit of the public by the
grantee, such as repairing the road or the like. But that was
not necessary here, for this toll was originally claimed by the
Crown itself, and therefore it could not commence by a grant
to itself."

That toll thorough requires consideration to be shown is
abundantly clear : see *King v. Corporation of Boston*, Sir W. J.,
162 ; *Hasport v. Wills*, 1 Mod. 47 ; *Warrington v. Moseley*,
4 Mod. 319 ; *Truman v. Walgham*, 2 Will. 298.

Just as a claim to have toll may be raised by prescription, so a man may prescribe to go quit of toll. The plea
should be in the affirmative, to go quit of toll, and not that
he had not paid toll. Fitzh., *N. B.*, Hale's Edit. p. 226, 14 H.
VI. 12.

Now with regard to prescription of Tithes: though tithes
be spiritual property yet most questions of prescription with
regard to them have been tried in the Temporal Courts. Co.
Litt. 96 b., Yelv. 92. But though this was so it appears that
spiritual persons were in a better position with regard to the

recovery of tithes or discharge from them than temporal persons. This was at Common Law: a change being afterwards made on the dissolution of the monasteries by the Statute 31 Hen. VIII.

Now the Common Law certainly affords a striking example of the anomaly brought about by the favour in which the Church was held. It appears best perhaps in the judgment of Hobart, C. J. in *Slade v. Drake*, Hob. 296.

" Now, touching the discharging of tythes themselves and the pleading of them at the Common Law it is to be observed that they are things of common right and do of right belong to the Church. And therefore though it be true that before the Council of Lateran, there were no parishes, nor parish priests that could claim them, but a man might give them to what spiritual person he would, yet to the church he must give them. Yet since parishes were created they are due to the parson or vicar of the parish. And therefore when you have a prohibition of discharge of tythes you must consider it as a plea in bar against common right, to a demand of tythes which is a common right.

" The Spiritual person had four ordinary ways of discharge, that is, first, Bull of the Pope : secondly, Composition : thirdly, Prescription, and these were absolute : fourthly, Order.

" Now clearly at the Common Law the Spiritual person could not claim his discharge by Bull, Composition or Order; but he must plead it with his ground and reason specially : but his discharge by *prescription was allowed him without any other reason because he was a person capable of such discharge.*

" Now temporal persons (not to speak of the king which was a special case, see **22** Ass.) had two ways to obtain Tythes, or to discharge Tythes. The first was by grant of the Parson, Patron or Ordinary; the other was by a *prescription : but that was ever not praescriptio simplex* but composita differing from the case of the spiritual persons.

" But now note a strange anomalum in this case, Tythes differing from all other cases in Law. For whereas Prescription and antiquity of time fortifies all other titles and supposeth the best beginning that Law can give them : in this case it

works clean contrary.   For whereas a grant of a Parson, Patron
or Ordinary is good of itself without any Recompense or Consideration, when it runs out to prescription it dies and perishes;
whereof no other reason is given, but that our books say that
a man may prescribe in modo decimandi, but not in non decimando: (2 Co. 44 b., note R. Dav. 6 b. accord).   (It was much
discussed whether the effect of 2 and 3 Will. IV. c. 100 was
to make every modus that had been paid for the specified time
good, or whether the effect was merely to shorten the time and
to leave the modus open to all other objections, as to rankness
&c.   The former appears to be the better opinion, see *Salkeld
v. Johnson*, 1 Hare, 210; 1 M. and G. 267; *Fellowes v. Clay*, 4
Q. B. 313; *Young v. Clare Hall*, 17 Q. B. 529.)   And this is
in favorem ecclesiae lest laymen should spoil the Church......
The Law presumes violently that a layman cannot be absolutely
discharged of Tithes; and therefore will not allow a prescription
of such discharge."   The effect of the Statute for the dissolution of Monasteries, 31 Hen. VIII. sec. 21, was to put the king
or the grantees of Church lands in the position of the prior
spiritual holders for purposes of discharge of tithes, so that
it would no longer be an answer, when, in a claim for tithes,
such holder pleaded that they were discharged by Bull, Composition or Order (the three modes open only to spiritual persons
before), to say that he was not a spiritual person: and it would
seem that if not before, at any rate by the effect of 2 and
3 Will. IV. c. 100, the prescription to be absolutely discharged
of tithes was opened to everyone.

The spiritual lands that were in these ways discharged of
tithes at the time of Henry VIII. were somewhat limited.   It
appears that originally all Abbots and Priors were subject to
the payment of tithes equally with other persons.   Pope Pascal
the Second exempted generally all the religious orders from payment of tithes in respect of lands in their own possession.   And
as to this it is to be observed that the lands were held to be
in their own possession when they were leased to non-spiritual
persons, since that was all in favour of the Church by reason
of the greater rent that could be claimed.   Cro. El. 785, Hob.
42.   The general discharge of Pascal was restrained by Pope

Hadrian IV. to the orders of Cistercians, Templars, and Hospitallers.

By the Lateran Council of 1215, the exemption ratione ordinis of religious houses was further restrained to those lands of which they were in possession before that Council. The Cistercians afterwards obtained bulls to exempt their lands that were leased in farms. But to obviate this practice it was enacted by Stat. 2 Hen. IV. c. 4, that all persons of that or any other order, religious or secular, who should put such bulls in execution, or should from thenceforth purchase such bulls, or by colour thereof should take advantage in any manner, should incur the penalties of praemunire. So that this Statute operated to prevent them from purchasing any such exemptions in future, but left their privileges untouched as they existed before it passed; applicable however only to such lands as they had before the Council of Lateran: consequently the lands obtained after that Council were not exempted. 3 Burn. *Ecc. L.* 416, 7th edit.; Toll. *Tith.* 171—174; Bac. *Abr. Tithes,* 2 Co. 44 b.

Now that a lay person cannot prescribe simply for tithes appears clear from the case of *Pigot v. Hern,* Cro. El. 599. There the Lord of the Manor of Prudshaw prescribed that he and his ancestors and all those whose estate he had &c. had used &c. to pay to the parson of Ovington £6 for all manner of tithes growing within the said parish: and that by reason thereof he and all those whose estate &c. used to have decimum cumulum garbarum—seu granorum of all his tenants within the said manor. There were two claims; one to be discharged of tithes; and the other to have them. It was held that both were good. As to the first being alleged in this special manner it was good. A Modus decimandi by the Lord of the Manor for himself and all the tenants of the manor is good, as it might have a legal commencement. But without such special matter alleged tithes which are spiritual things and due jure divino for the recovery of which before 2 and 3 Ed. VI. c. 7 remedy lay only in the Spiritual Court, and there was no remedy at Common Law, cannot be prescribed for generally by a man in him and all those whose estate he has, *Winchcomb's Case,* Cro. El.

293. Nor can they be parcel or appurtenant to a manor or any other temporal inheritance. *Bishop of Winchester's Case*, 2 Rep. 45 b.

As regards the second prescription in *Pigot v. Hern, ubi sup.*, it was held to be good if properly pleaded. Thus if the Lord pleads to have decimas garbarum that is ill : for it is a claim for tithes which a layman cannot have "because he is not capable of them in regard they be spiritual." But if he pleads to have decimam garbam that is merely a claim to a temporal profit a prendre and is good : and may well be parcel of a manor.

But with regard to this the king is in a different position. For as in 22 Ass. 75 the king, if Lord of the Manor, may prescribe to have tithes; for he is capable of them though they be spiritual; being mixta persona et capax spiritualis jurisdictionis. The Law as to discharge of tithes is very succinctly put by Sir W. Jones, in his report of the case of *Lydowne v. Holme*, W. J. 368.

Of something the same nature as a prescription in modo decimandi was the case of *Wise v. Green*, Freem. Rep. 468. There a man prescribed that by reason of repairing a Chapel of Ease he had been time out of mind exempted from contributing towards the repairs of the church : and this was held a good prescription.

In this connexion of things ecclesiastical it may be well to notice the claim to pews in a parish church by prescription.

Now prima facie the Ordinary has the legal right to arrange the seats in the church as he thinks best, and most in conformity with the rights of the parishioners, but that right may be qualified by a legal prescriptive right which any of the parishioners may have acquired in derogation of such general right. Now any parishioner may, by faculty from the Ordinary, receive the right to a particular pew, as appurtenant to a certain messuage; but even the Ordinary cannot grant a seat appurtenant to lands. *Pettman v. Bridger*, 1 Phillim. *Eccl.* 316. But mere possession is not enough. "To exclude the Ordinary from his jurisdiction it is necessary not merely that a possession should be shown for many years, but that the pew should have been built and repaired time out of mind." Phillim. *Eccl. Law*, Vol. II. p. 1800. How long possession was required does not seem quite plain, since Lord Penzance in *Crisp v. Martin*, L. R., 2 P. D., at p. 25, says, "It is necessary to show a user more or less extended of the pew (*I say more or less because I do not find anywhere a very definite period laid down during which it must have existed*), but it is also necessary to prove that he or those under whom he claims have taken upon themselves in relief of the parish, the burthen of repairing it." I think the indefiniteness of the period may be accounted for in this way. Of course at Common Law a prescriptive claim to a pew must as regards time be the same as any other prescription; but claims to pews would be settled in the generality of cases in the Spiritual Courts which did not proceed on strictly legal grounds and the jurisdiction of which was ousted when any strictly legal claim arose for decision. This appears clear from *Slade v. Drake*, Hob. 296, where the Chief Justice speaks as follows: "For this is regular for difference between the king's Courts and the Courts Ecclesiastical, that though a spiritual cause cannot originally and primitively fall into the king's Court; as for calling a man heretic he shall not have an action of the case (20 H. VIII.). Yet if a civil action be well commenced as in the cases cited, a Quare impedit, or an action of false imprisonment, if anything fall incidentally that is spiritual the king's Court shall continue the plea on it either by jury or demurrer, except in the case where the law hath provided trial by ecclesiastics, as by the issue upon Bastardy umques accouple &c., literature and the like: in which case the Bishops are not judges, but ministers of the king's Courts as other kind of triers are: whereupon the Court proceeds to judgment according to their certificates and trials. *But on the contrary if a case begin well in the Spiritual Court as being spiritual, and a point fall incidentally that is of temporal cognisance it is clean contrary:* for the trial is called from them as in daily experience in prescription and limits of parishes in suits of Tythes."

The question what length of possession is required in the spiritual courts, and what length when the case was in the ordinary Courts of law appears well in the judgment of Sir John Nicoll in *Pettman v. Bridger*, 1 Phillim. *Eccl.* 316, where the distinction appears. He says, "A possessory right is not good against the Churchwardens and the Ordinary—they may displace and make new arrangements but they ought not without cause to displace persons in possession; if they do the Ordinary would reinstate them—the possession therefore will have its weight—the Ordinary would give a person in possession ceteris paribus the preference over a mere stranger. A possessory right is sufficient to maintain a suit against a mere disturber. A prescriptive right" (coming now to a claim at Common Law) "must be clearly proved....In the first place it is necessary to show that use and occupation of the seat *has been from time immemorial* appurtenant to a certain messuage." I do not think therefore that there is any ground for saying that a prescription for a pew is any different in point of time from any ordinary prescription.

There is a case, *Knapp v. Parishioners of Willesden*, in 2 Roberts, *Eccl.* 358, which seems rather to negative the necessity of repairs in a prescriptive claim to a pew. But that was a case where no necessity for repairs had arisen, and therefore the claimant was not to be in any worse position.

It does not appear to have ever been absolutely decided whether a claim to a pew comes under the Prescription Act. Lord Penzance, however, in *Crisp v. Martin, sup.* expressed his opinion that it did not.

A somewhat similar right is the right of burial. Thus Com. Dig., *Cemetery*, says, "So a man may prescribe that he is tenant of an ancient messuage and ought to have separate burial in such a vault within the Church, or in such an isle or the quire." And if he be disturbed he may have an action on the case— 2 Cro. 606.

But a custom that every parishioner has a right to bury his dead relations in the churchyard as near to their ancestors as possible is bad. 2 Wils. 28.

But it is difficult to see how a prescription will lie for burial in a church. For according to *Bryan v. Whistler*, 8 B. and C. 295, such a right cannot be granted. That is to say, only the parson has the power to grant a right of burial in the church. For as is said in *Francis v. Ley*, Cro. Jac. 366,

"Neither the Ordinary himself nor the Churchwardens can grant license of burying to any within the church, but the parson only, because the soil and freehold of the church is only in the parson and in none other." And although in Gibson's *Codex*, p. 542, this is denied to be the true reason, as it would apply equally to the churchyard; yet another reason equally valid is given, viz. that the ecclesiastical laws have appointed the incumbent as the proper judge of the fitness or unfitness of any particular person to have the privilege of burial in the church. Hence it is clear that only the parson can grant the right of burial in the church.

And from *Bryan v. Whistler, sup.*, it appears that such grant can only be made by deed, and *is limited to the particular instance, and cannot be* a general grant of the privilege of burial.

Bayley, J., there says (p. 293), "The rector has the freehold of the church for public purposes, not for his own emolument; to supply places for burial from time to time as the necessities of his parish require, and not to grant away vaults."

There are some interesting cases upon prescriptions in restraint of trade. Thus in *Sir George Farmer's Case*, 8 Rep. 125 b, a prescription was laid to bake bread for all the inhabitants of Northampton and to prevent anyone else doing so. And this was adjudged a reasonable prescription by Sir Chs. May et totam curiam.

This may be supported on the ground that all the tenements were held of the manor, and the grant may have been on that condition. There is, however, another report of the case in Owen, p. 67, where the result is stated to be the direct contrary.

But a prescription of a wider nature would not have been allowed since it could not have been expressly granted. Thus in a case of *Darcy v. Allen*, cited in 8 Rep. 125, where the plaintiff claimed that Queen Elizabeth granted that he should have the sole traffic with playing cards, and should only import them from beyond the sea into this kingdom, also that he should have the sole making of playing cards in this kingdom, it was adjudged bad.

Guston v. Shittington, cited D. 279 b, p. 10 ; Vin. Ab., *Presc.*, 261, was a case of trespass for taking goods. The defendant justified as a servant of the Corporation of York, and said that time out of mind there had been a custom to seize wares foreign bought and foreign sold within the liberty of the City of York as forfeited ; and that the said goods were wares foreign bought and foreign sold. And this was held a good prescription. It is said that this prescription is bad as directly contrary to the Statute of 9 Ed. III. c. 5, which stated that upon things disclosed to him being found to the great oppression of the realm, the king in his Parliament had ordained that all Merchants, Strangers and denizens, might sell all manner of things vendible at what place soever, be it city, borough, &c., within franchise or without, and provided penalties for breach. This Statute did evidently meet the case : but it also clearly shows that prior to the Statute such a prescription would have been good.

Perhaps the most important, at any rate in early times, of the rights that could be prescribed for, and certainly among the most historically interesting, are rights of common. An essay upon prescription would therefore be obviously incomplete without treating of rights of common. But rights of common are a subject that require an essay of no mean dimensions to themselves. And the difficulty when one once begins is to know where to stop. Time will not allow me to deal in anything like an adequate manner with rights of common : but I must give just such an outline as will show generally what was claimable by prescription. I treat the subject in a cursory manner with the less regret because there is an admirable book upon them by the late Mr Joshua Williams, published in 1877. Now it will clear the ground to deal at once with common appendant. With that prescription is not concerned. It has been shown by Sir Henry Maine (*Village Communities*), and by Mr Joshua Williams, *Commons*, p. 37 seq., how common appendant became incident to the possession of certain lands. And though they have shown that common appendant arose out of the system of cultivation practised in village communities prior to the Manorial System, and that therefore there may be common appendant, as a relic of that prior system, in wastes other than those of the lord of the particular manor, yet of course the fact still remains that common appendant is an incident of such possession, and does not require or admit of prescription. See Bro. Abr., *Prescript.* p. 39 : Y.-B. 21 H. VII. 53.

We have left then Common Appurtenant, and Common in gross. Common appurtenant is claimed by express grant, or by prescription in a que estate. We shall see in what cases it can become common in gross. Common in gross whether arising out of a prior common appurtenant, or created in gross is prescribed for in gross. Certainly the most important of rights of common were common of pasture, and I shall speak, at any rate at first, with reference to those.

Now common appurtenant may be claimed by express grant, *Bradshaw v. Eyre*, Cro. Eliz. 570, or by what looks very like a prescription by presumption of modern lost grant, but seems to have been treated merely as a presumption of grant, *Cowlam v. Slack*, 15 East, 108, or by prescription ; and this either from time of legal memory, or under the prescription Act by enjoyment for 30 years, or 60 years to become indefeasible. Though of course even then the right must be such an one as could lawfully be granted, or it will not become established by any length of enjoyment, see *Mill v. Commrs. of New Forest*, 18 C. B. 60 ; *A.-G. v. Mathias*, 4 K. and J. 579.

Common appurtenant was a much wider right than common appendant. It might extend to other beasts. Only commonable beasts, *i.e.* beasts of the plough, horses or oxen, or animals that manure the land, cows or sheep, can be put to pasture in right of common appendant, while other beasts may in right of common appurtenant. Common appendant was originally only in respect of beasts levant and couchant upon the land, though it was afterwards in some cases stinted to a certain fixed number, while common appurtenant though frequently in respect of beasts levant and couchant, was not necessarily so, even at the first grant. One large right was that of common of pasture enjoyed by all owners and occupiers of lands within a forest, as some compensation for the hardship of the forest rights. This right extended to all the waste lands in the forest, and not merely to those of the particular manor of which their tenements were held. *Commrs. of Sewers v. Glasse*, L. R. 19 Eq. 134.

Now these rights of common extended equally to every part of the waste, and therefore though it were more than sufficient for all those claiming common over it, the lords were prevented from doing anything with it.

To remedy this the Statute of Merton, 20 Hen. III. c. 4, provided that an assise should be held to determine the sufficiency of the common, and if there was more than enough that the lords should be free to approve and make their profit of the residue.

It was much discussed whether this Statute gave any new right to the lord or was merely in affirmance of the common law. Williams after considering the question comes to the conclusion (p. 108) that " so far as the statute enabled lords who had granted the usual common appendant over their wastes to derogate from their grants by enclosing a portion of the waste, so far the statute gave a new authority which the lord had not before. But so far as the statute extended to common acquired merely by user, of which there must have been a large quantity in those days, so far very probably at Common Law the lord had a power to improve by enclosure provided he left sufficiency for the Commoners." Now the Statute of Merton applied only to cases between lord and tenant. The Stat. West. II., 13 Ed. I. c. 46, was passed to extend the right of approvement of a waste against persons having rights of common there who were not tenants of the lord desiring to approve.

Those Statutes, it has been decided, apply to common appurtenant, *Robinson v. Maharajah Duleep Singh*, 11 Ch. D. 822, but they do not apply to common in gross, Co. 2*nd Inst.* pt. 2, p. 475.

The onus is on the lord to show that there is sufficient common left.

The Commons Act, 1876, has somewhat restricted the right of approvement under the earlier statutes by providing that when any enclosure is intended otherwise than under the provisions of that Act, notice shall be given by advertisement in the local papers three months beforehand.

Curious as it may seem, it was only the other day that the question of what was meant by sufficiency of common was decided by the Court of Appeal. That was in the case of *Robertson v. Hartopp*, 43 Ch. D. 484.

That was an action brought on behalf of the tenants of the Manor of Banstead to restrain the lord from enclosing parts of the waste and from digging or removing any part of the soil of the waste so as to interfere with their rights of common. It was proved that the tenants had rights of common of pasturage appendant over the wastes for sheep, and that certain landowners, not tenants of the manor, had rights of common appurtenant over it for sheep, and that such rights appendant and appurtenant entitled the commoners to turn out on the waste a greater number of sheep, measured by levancy and couchancy upon their tenements, than the waste would carry. But it was also shown that having regard to the average number of sheep which had been turned out for many years it was highly improbable that nearly as many sheep as the waste could carry would ever be turned out upon it. But the Court of Appeal held, affirming the decision of Stirling, J., that the question of sufficiency was to be determined not according to the average number of sheep actually turned out, but according to the aggregate number the commoners were entitled to turn out.

But a doubt was expressed whether in determining the fact whether there was sufficiency for the aggregate number of sheep the commoners were entitled to turn out, regard should not be had to the modern system of farming whereby the sheep do not get all their sustenance from the common. *Lascelles v. Lord Onslow*, 2 Q. B. D. 433.

This right of approvement exists only against common of pasture, Co. 2nd *Inst.* pt. 1, p. 86. But notwithstanding the existence of other rights of common, *e.g.* of piscary, turbary, estovers or the like, the lord may enclose, so long as he does not hinder their exercise. *Hall v. Byron*, 4 Ch. D. 680 ; *Fawcett v. Strickland*, Willes, p. 61. And he may by custom, though not under the statutes, approve against other rights of common ; *Lascelles v. Lord Onslow*, 2 Q. B. Div. 433 ; *Arlett v. Ellis*, 7 B. and C. 436.

There have been other Acts enabling enclosure for various purposes, and many decisions turning generally on the special provisions of the Acts in question. Thus 51 Geo. III. c. 115, par. 2, allows approvement for a church, &c. But it only speaks of approvement as against rights of common, and therefore when the inhabitants claimed a custom to play all lawful sports and games upon the land proposed to be enclosed, which is a good custom, *Abbot v. Weekly*, 1 Lev. 176, it was held (*Forbes v. Eccl. Comms. of England*, L. R., 5 Eq. 51), that the enclosure was not authorised by the Act. See too *Hall v. Nottingham*, L. R., 1 Ex. D. 1.

Common in gross may be prescribed for by a man or his ancestors as having been always common in gross. Or it may be prescribed for partly in a que estate and partly in a man and his ancestors. This would be the case where the common had originally been gained as appurtenant to a tenement and after-wards become in gross by the owner of the tenement alienating either the right of common or the tenement and reserving the other. But it is to be observed that this separation of the common from the tenement could only be made when the common had ceased to be for cattle levant and couchant upon the tenement and had been changed into, or had originally been created as common for a fixed number of cattle.

Drury v. Kent, Cro. Jac. 14.

Spooner v. Day, Cro. Car. 432.

Daniel v. Hanslip, 2 Lev. 67.

In the second of those cases it is clearly laid down that where the common, though appurtenant, is or has become certain, it may well be granted away, or annexed to part of the tenement, since it cannot become a greater charge than before.

Common in gross is not affected by the Statutes of Merton and Westminster II. (Coke, *Inst.* 2nd pt. cap. 46, p. 475). Of course where the common in gross was for an unlimited number of cattle, as it might be, no approvement could be possible, leaving a sufficiency. But when the common in gross was for a certain number one cannot see why, since the evil to be remedied was the same, the Statutes should not have been made to extend to it. And it has further been decided (*Shuttleworth v. Le Fleming*, 19 C. B., N. S. 687) that the prescription Act does not apply to easements or profits in gross.

It may be as well here to notice a point of very great importance as limiting the rights that may be prescribed for. It is not by any means every kind of right that can be prescribed for; and some rights can only be claimed as appurtenant to a tenement, and some only in gross.

Thus in English Law it is not open to an owner to annex new incidents to the tenure of his land. Therefore with regard to easements such as a right of way, which can only be of value as being attached to and connected with the enjoyment of a dominant tenement, it has been held (*Ackroyd v. Smith*, 10 C. B. 186) that such rights can only be created as appurtenant to a tenement, and that they cannot be granted and therefore cannot be prescribed for in gross.

Conversely with regard to profits which may be valuable quite irrespective of the ownership of any tenement it has been held, see *Bailey v. Stephens*, 12 C. B., N. S. 114, and *Sir Francis Barrington's Case*, 8 Rep. 136, that when such a right has no reference to user upon and for the benefit of a dominant tenement it is not and cannot be appurtenant to a tenement, and therefore does not pass by a grant of the tenement; though it may be created in gross and therefore prescribed for in gross. And of course a profit for the benefit of a tenement such as estovers of house bote, or common for *cattle levant and couchant* may be created and prescribed for as appurtenant to a tenement. The Court therefore held in *Bailey v. Stephens, sup.* that a claim of a right as appurtenant to a tenement to enter another close and cut all the wood growing thereon could not have been granted as appurtenant, and therefore the claim was bad. It must not be forgotten that while a profit may be created and prescribed for in gross, yet that a profit appurtenant for *e.g.* cattle levant and couchant cannot be granted away in gross so long as it is for cattle levant and couchant, though it may so soon as the number of cattle is fixed. And that though a profit such as common sans nombre cannot be created as appurtenant to a tenement, but may be created in gross and prescribed for in gross: yet where it is unlimited in this way, though grantable, it is not assignable, and therefore must be prescribed for in a man and his own ancestors, and not in the ancestors of someone else and through them by grant to the claimant. *Weekly v. Wildman*, Lord Raym. 407.

Now as regards a profit that may be granted either as appurtenant or in gross it appears that, while, if it be so large as not to be merely for the benefit of the tenement, it cannot be appurtenant, the rule is equally positive in the converse. So that if a profit be granted apparently in gross, but for supplying the needs of a given tenement it is made appurtenant to that tenement. Thus in *Sym's Case*, 8 Rep. 54 A, it is said " if a man be seised of a house in the right of his wife and another grants to the husband and his heirs to have sufficient estovers, to burn in the same house, in that case the estovers are appurtenant to the house and shall descend to the issue of the husband and wife. So if one has a house on the part of his mother, and one grants to him, that he and his heirs shall have competent house bote to be burnt in the same house, this is appurtenant to the house; and although it be a new purchase, yet it shall go with the house to the heir of the part of the mother."

There was a curious case of prescription for common, *Hill v. Ellard*, Lev. 141, Sid. 226. There in (as Siderfin has it, Replevin dun cow) Replevin the issue was upon a prescription for every yardland within such a vill to have common for 12 cows, and for a quarter of a yardland common for 3, and for half a quarter for a cow and a half. And the prescription was for four cows and a half, and verdict for the plaintiff. And it was moved in arrest of judgment that the issue was senseless and void, for there could not be common for half a cow. But it was held that in any case, though the prescription might not be able to stand as to the four and a half, yet that as the damage was by one cow and the prescription found for four and a half, there was enough to serve the turn of the person prescribing. And it would seem that after verdict at any rate, the prescription would be upheld by assuming that it was common for a cow for half a year; or that two men had but one cow, and each claimed common for half a cow.

I shall pass in the most cursory manner over Easements which have been fully dealt with by Mr Gale and Mr Goddard. Now an easement has been defined in *Termes de la Ley*, p. 284 to be "a privilege that one neighbour hath of another by writing or prescription without profit as a way or sink through the land or such like." That seems to me a good general definition. The definition given by Mr Goddard is fuller and more accurate. It is really an explanation of the old definition by the light of subsequent decisions. His definition is:—

"An easement is a privilege without profit which the owner of one tenement has a right to enjoy in respect of that tenement in or over the tenement of another person, by reason whereof the latter is obliged to suffer or refrain from doing something on his own tenement for the advantage of the former."

It is my duty to show how the nature of easements requires this further explanation. But I shall content myself by giving concisely the results arrived at by Mr Goddard, through his longer exposition.

In the first place it is material to notice the definition that the privilege is one held *by writing* or prescription. At that time a writing in law meant a document under Seal. Now an easement is an incorporeal hereditament, and grantable only by deed. If so granted it holds good for ever, and passes by a proper conveyance of the dominant tenement. If the right be granted merely by writing (without Seal), that is a mere personal license to the licensee which cannot be granted away by him, and which it will be at once seen is a very different thing from a grant of the easement.

It is convenient to make another distinction. There are certain easements which do not arise without grant express or implied by the owner of the servient tenement. There are others, which in most respects do not in their incidents and in the law applicable to them differ from such easements; but which, without any grant of the owner, are by law annexed to the land. It is convenient to call them natural rights for the purpose of distinguishing them, because in one important particular the law as to them differs from that applicable to easements arising by grant. Easements arising by grant may be suspended or extinguished, but natural rights can only be suspended for a time, greater or less according to circumstances, and upon the removal of the obstacle they revive proprio vigore.

Thus in *Sury v. Pigot*, Popham, 166; Tudor's L. C. on R. P., Whitlock, J., says:—" A way or common shall be extinguished because they are part of the profits of the land, and the same law is of fisheries also, but in our case the watercourse doth not begin by the consent of the parties, nor by prescription, but ex jure naturae, and therefore shall not be extinguished by unity." This is approved of in *Wood v. Waud*, 3 Ex. 775 and numerous other cases.

Now it is to be observed first that an easement is defined to be a privilege. It is not a right to the soil but a right of doing something with respect to it. It is a privilege without profit. If the right consists in a right to take something from the servient land that is a profit a prendre, unless the right be to enter land and take away water not yet appropriated and made the property of anybody; for water is not the property of anybody until confined in a vessel. See *Race v. Ward*, 4 E. and B. 702. *Mainwaring v. Wasdale*, 5 A. and E. 758.

On the other hand it is always necessary to look to the substance of the right and not to the mere form in which it is granted. It is a privilege in the land of another, therefore if the right granted be so large that it gives power to take away the whole substance of the land, or to exclude the grantor, then it is no longer to be considered an easement, but is a grant of the land. Thus if a right be granted to take coal from under the land of the grantor, that is a privilege, and an incorporeal hereditament; but if it be to take all the coal under a particular close that is no longer a privilege at all, but is a grant of the particular stratum of the land.

See *Sanders v. Norwood*, Cro. Eliz. 683 where Granville, J., makes the distinction.

So in *Busyard v. Capel*, 8 B. and C. 141; 6 Bing. 150, it was held that a grant of the exclusive use of the land reserving the land, was a grant of the land, and not a mere easement.

See too *Roads v. Parish of Trumpington*, L. R. 6 Q. B. 56.

The general rule that no easement can be so extensive as to exclude the grantee entirely from the use of his land was laid down in *Dyer v. Lady James Hay*, 1 Macq. 305, where it is said that "neither by the Law of Scotland nor of England can there be a prescriptive right in the nature of a servitude or easement so large as to preclude the ordinary user of property by the owner of the lands affected." Again it is to be observed that a right in gross is not properly an easement, which requires a dominant and servient tenement. This requirement is, I take it, adverted to in the definition in *Termes de la Ley* as "the privilege which one *neighbour hath of another.*" It follows that an easement belonging to a dominant tenement cannot be severed from it or granted to a person in gross; and a personal right granted to one man cannot be granted over by him to another. *Ackroyd v. Smith*, 10 C. B. 164.

The point has been fought out over the question of a right of a riparian owner to grant away to a non-riparian owner part of his natural right of user of the water of a stream. It was argued that this natural right is just the same as any other right, the subject of property, and therefore must possess the natural incident of property, assignability. But this argument is based upon the fallacy of regarding the right of a riparian owner as an ordinary right of property. It is a right attached by the law to the ownership of the soil, and therefore should not exist severed from the soil. As is said by Bowen, L. J., in *Ormond v. Todmorden Mill Co.*, 11 Q. B. D. 172, "I incline to think that the rights of a riparian proprietor are inseparably attached to the soil." In that case *Potter v. Stockport Water-works Co.* 3 H. and C. 300 was directly approved. There the law had been laid down thus. "It seems to us clear that the rights which a riparian proprietor has with respect to the water are entirely derived from his possession of land abutting on the river. If he grants away any portion of his land so abutting then the grantee becomes a riparian proprietor and has similar rights. But if he grants away a portion of his estate not abutting on the river, then clearly the grantee of the land would have no water rights by virtue merely of his occupation. Can he have them by express grant? It seems to us that the true answer to this is that he can have them against the grantor, but not so as to sue other persons in his own name for an infringement of them."

It is now quite clear that if the rights of the other riparian owners are sensibly affected they can obtain an injunction against the grantee of the riparian owners. That appears in the cases cited. It is also clear that if the rights of other riparian owners are not affected, as when water, though taken, is returned uninjured and undiminished, they cannot obtain an injunction. *Kensit v. Great Eastern Railway Co.,* 27 Ch. D. 122. That is if it be the case that not only is there no immediate injury sustained, but when there is also no probability of an injury accruing from a continuance of the abstraction. And it appears that the burden of proving that no future injury can arise, lies upon those who are doing the acts which it is alleged might lead to an injury.

There is a very important matter to be borne in mind in considering the nature of easements. An easement must be annexed to a dominant tenement; and it is only allowed by the law to be so annexed, upon the analogy of covenants that run with the land, when the user of it is connected with and beneficial to the dominant tenement, and is, at the same time, an incident of an ordinary kind known to the Law. For, as Lord Brougham said in *Keppel v. Bailey,* 2 Myl. and K. 517, the case upon covenants running with the land "Incidents of a novel kind cannot be devised and attached to property at the fancy and caprice of any owner."

And it was distinctly held in *Ackroyd v. Smith,* 10 C. B. 164, that it is not competent to a vendor to create rights unconnected with the use or enjoyment of the land, and to annex them to it. Neither can the owner of land render it subject to new species of burden so as to bind it in the hands of an assignee.

H.   9

Ackroyd v. Smith was referred to and explained in *Thorpe v. Brumfitt*, 8 Ch. 655; but the principle then laid down was not in the least found fault with, the explanation referring only to the construction of a grant of a right of way. See too *Hill v. Tupper*, 32 L. J. Ex. 217, *Ellis v. Mayor &c., of Bridgnorth*, 32 L. J. C. P. 273.

The necessity of the connection with the dominant tenement is strongly brought out in *Bailey v. Stevens*, 31 L. J., C. P. 226. That was a claim by prescription by the tenant of land to cut down timber on other land, but the plea did not claim that the timber was to be used in any way upon the dominant tenement. It was held that the right could not be annexed to the land so as to be enjoyed by the occupier as such, or be claimed by prescription. Byles, J., says, "How can such a right as this be retained by the occupier of land as such? It is in no way connected with the enjoyment of the land occupied. A man might as well try to make a right of way over land in Kent appurtenant to an estate in Northumberland."

Of course all the cases which show that a riparian owner on a stream is only entitled to take the water of the stream for reasonable use upon his land come within, and might also be decided upon this same principle, viz., that an user unconnected with the enjoyment of the dominant tenement cannot be annexed to its occupation. As to this, see among other cases, *Earl of Sandwich v. Great Northern Ry. Co.*, 49 L. J. Ch. 225. *Swindon Water Works Co. (Ld.) v. Wilts and Berks Canal Co.*, L. R. 7 Eng. and Ir. App. 697.

I shall advert hereafter to the principle laid down in *Mason v. Hereford and Shrewsbury Ry. Co.*, L. R. 6 Q. B. 578, that when an easement had incidentally also been beneficial to the servient tenement, that fact gives no right to the owner of the servient tenement to have the user by the owner of the dominant tenement continued, even though the cessation of user may bring about a positive injury to the servient tenement.

Finally, it must be carefully borne in mind that an Easement is a right to the dominant owner to do something, either on his own or the servient tenement, or constituting an obligation upon the servient owner to refrain from doing something on his own tenement that he would otherwise be entitled to do: but it in no case creates any obligation on the servient owners to actively do something. Of course the principle of *Tulk v. Moxhay* of the obligation of a covenant upon a person taking with notice of it, is now so clearly restricted to negative covenants (see *Haywood v. Brunswick Building Society*, 8 Q. B. D. 403, and *L. and S. W. Ry. Co. v. Gomm*, 20 Ch. D. 562) that there can be no ground for attempting to force upon a servient owner any positive obligation under that principle.

It must be observed that where an easement is acquired the owner of the easement has thereby a right to enter the servient tenement and repair that part of it over which the easement is enjoyed. For as is said in *Pomfret v. Ricroft*, 1 Saund. 320: "when the use of a thing is granted everything is granted by which the grantee may enjoy such use." It was then held that when a man had the use of a pump upon another's land he might enter or repair it, but that the owner was not bound to keep it in repair.

So in *Macclesfield Highway Board v. Grant*, 51 L. J., Q. B. 357, it was held that the owner of a wall from which a highway had gained a right of support was not bound to repair it, but that the Highway board might.

So in *Chauntler v. Robinson*, 4 Ex. 163, it was held that the owner of a house, subject to an easement of support, was not bound to repair it; he was only bound to prevent it being a nuisance. And in *Duncan v. Louch*, 6 Q. B. 909, the principle was again affirmed of the right to repair, it being there held that people who had a right to walk on the "Terrace Walk" had thereby a right to repair it.

There is another point of importance to be noticed before quitting the things of which prescription may be made. Prescription is a matter of time and long endurance. No prescription therefore can be made in respect of any subject matter that is not of a continuing and permanent character. Thus in *Maberley v. Dowson*, 5 L. J., K. B. 261, where a tenant had erected a building upon strong posts or pillars fixed into stone plinths, which stone plinths rested upon brickwork, and had enjoyed light coming into a window in such building for 27 years, and then had the light obstructed by the defendant, it was held that no prescriptive right had been gained. It was said that when a window has been opened in a building erected by a tenant for the mere purpose of trade, and which is not annexed to the freehold, but may be removed by the tenant at his pleasure, or at the end of his term, no prescriptive right can be gained, since the temporary nature of the structure prevents the presumption of a grant by the servient owner. And the principle has been thoroughly established in the case of artificial water courses, it having been decided that where an artificial watercourse is constructed to be permanent, prescriptive rights may be gained over it, but when it is created merely for a temporary purpose no such rights can be acquired. See *Arkwright v. Gell*, 5 M. and W. 503. It is to be observed, however, that this applies in its strictness only to the person who constructs the artificial watercourse. Prescriptive rights may sometimes be acquired against other persons through whose land the artificial stream flows, when they cannot against the originator. (See *Wood v. Waud*, 3 Ex. at p. 780.)

When, however, the stream, though artificial, is of a permanent character, there can be no reason why a grant should not be presumed. See *Wood v. Waud*, 3 Ex. 798.

Of course, if the stream, though artificial, be polluted, even by its creator, that is quite a different question. That constitutes a trespass by bringing foul matter upon the plaintiff's land. See a case of this kind, not against the person in whose land the stream commenced, but against some one through whose land it passed.

Major v. Chadwick, 11 A. and E. 571.

The question whether the stream in question is temporary or permanent is, of course, a question of fact in each case. The decision as to the fact must depend upon several elements. The mere length of time during which the stream has continued or is likely to continue, is not the sole element in the case. The test is rather the intention of the party creating it, to be inferred from the purpose for which it is made to flow, the mode in which it is created, the length of time it has continued, and any other special circumstances. See two recent cases in which this question has been considered with opposite results:—*Chamber Colliery Co. v. Hopwood*, 32 Ch. D. 554. *Rameshen Preshad Raiain Serigh v. Kooing Behari Pattuk*, 4 App. Cas. 121.

CHAPTER V.

How Prescription must be made: the Requisites of Prescription.

THE first point to be noted here is that unlike Roman Law, where a justus titulus was required to found usucapio, English Law allows Prescription to run in every case where possession has been taken, even by trespass, and the right has been exercised openly by the possessor as his own. I merely point out this distinction here but do not elaborate it, because the nature of English Prescription will appear in the instances adduced throughout.

Another thing to notice under this head is that the prescription must either be actually certain, or what is equivalent to certainty, capable of being rendered certain by reference to something else, upon the principle id certum est quod certum reddi potest. Thus a prescription for common for cattle levant and couchant is certain, for the number of cattle levant and couchant is determinable by reference to the tenement. The way in which the number of cattle properly levant and couchant upon a tenement was determined, or where the common was insufficient for all the cattle levant and couchant upon the tenements having common in that waste, the method in which the proportionate abatement for each tenement was settled, was by the writ of admeasurement of pasture. This according to Blackstone, 21st edit., Vol. III. p. 238, " lies either where a common appurtenant or in gross is certain as to number, or where a man has common appendant or appurtenant to his land, the quantity of which common has never yet been ascertained. In either of these cases as well the lord or any of the commoners is entitled to this writ of admeasurement.

This writ of admeasurement was abolished by Stat. 3 and 4 Will. IV. c. 27 along with the other real actions. The remedy now is for the Lord by distraint or trespass, and for a commoner an action on the case. *Cape v. Scott*, L. R. 9 Q. B. 269. Blackstone apparently does not consider that the writ would lie where there was one commoner who had common sans nombre : but I cannot help thinking that it was the existence of this writ that made common sans nombre, so far as it existed, permissible at all. It is not, perhaps, absolutely precluded by the requirement for a prescription to be certain, since the number might be said to be determined by the will of the commoner : he could put on as many as he chose.

In the note to this writ in Fitzherbert's *Natura Brevium*, p. 125, it is stated that the writ will not lie for *common appendant* or for *common by specialty sans nombre*. But the authority there given is 22 Ass. 55, which certainly does not bear out the note. And in the case of *Mellor v. Spateman*, 1 Saund. 346 d., it was definitely held that there cannot be any such thing as common in gross without number, and the plea was in that case held bad for want of words, making the claim one for cattle levant and couchant.

On the other hand in *Weekly v. Wildman*, Lord Raym., at p. 407, it is said both by Powell and Treby, J.J. that a common sans nombre could be created, though it was not grantable over.

I think therefore that the only way to reconcile these apparently conflicting opinions is as follows :—

It is evident that levancy and couchancy are incident to common appendant and appurtenant.

Benson v. Chester, 8 T. R. 396.

Bennet v. Reeve, Willes, 232.

But these were reducible to a fixed number upon a writ of admeasurement.

I think it must be held that common in gross sans nombre could be granted, *Weekly v. Wildman, sup.* and that what is meant in *Mellor v. Spateman, sup.* by saying that there cannot be any common in gross sans number, is that common sans number is subject to the writ of admeasurement. I cannot find any authority that it is not. That it should be so subject is certainly agreeable to the requirement that a prescription must be certain. And although it may well be that a common sans nombre was rare, yet it is improbable that if it had not been reducible to reasonable limits some more definite authority upon the subject would not be existing and well known.

It seems that when action is brought for surcharging the common though all commoners are admeasured, yet those who are not made defendants, as not having surcharged, cannot be admeasured to their prejudice, 8 H. VI. 26. Of course where the lord distrained the surcharging cattle, the only way to determine whether they were surcharging the common was an admeasurement. It seems too that where only two inter-common on one another's lands, the writ does not lie, the remedy there being by assise as terretenant. But where there are three who so intercommon, the writ does lie, 18 E. III. 43. As further illustrating the requirement of certainty, may be cited *Hayward v. Cunnington*, 1 Lev. 231. There in trespass for digging turfs the Defendant pleads that he is seised of an ancient house and prescribes to have so many turfs every year as two men could dig in a day, as belonging to his messuage. The Plaintiff demurs, for that " 'tis not shown that the turfs were to be burnt in his house, and all estovers are to be used in the house, and as it is laid here they may be sold although he claims them as appurtenant to his house:" and a case was cited that a prescription for digging clay in another's soil to make pots, is void, which Kelynge, C.J., remembered: "but 'twas answered and resolved, that when the thing is uncertain as estovers, it ought to be applied to the house to ascertain it; but here it is certain enough in itself, viz. so much as two men could dig in a day:" and for authorities were cited Rastell's Entries, 539 and 1 Cro. *Spooner v. Day*. And judgment was given for the plaintiff.

So again if the tenants of a Manor prescribe that they ought not to pay a fine for renewing their copyhold estates more than two years' rent, but ought to pay a fine of two years' rent or less, this is not a good prescription for the uncertainty; for sometimes they are to pay two years' rent and sometimes less. *Greene v. Bury*, Vin. Ab., *Prescrip.* 203.

So if a man prescribes to pay a penny or thereabouts for

Tithes of every acre of arable land, this is not a good prescription for the uncertainty. *Allen's Case*, Vin. Ab., *Prescrip.* 203.

A Prescription to be good must be reasonable:—This requirement, it will be at once seen, reduces in a very material degree what might have hitherto appeared the illimitable extent of a prescription. The working of the requirement will be best seen in its application to some of the instances already adduced.

Tolls afford a striking illustration of its application. In *Lawrence v. Hitch*, L. R. 3 Q. B. 521, a toll of 1/- for every waggon, cart, horse or ass load of fruit or vegetables brought into and hawked about the town of Cheltenham, was claimed by prescription from the time of legal memory. The toll had been collected regularly as of right from 1810 to 1863. But in a case in which the Court was to draw inferences of fact, the objection was taken that this toll was rank, that is, was of an amount that could not reasonably have been claimed in the time of Richard I. But the Court held upon the facts that 1/- a load was not unreasonable even for that time; though it was not necessary for the decision so to hold, since the Court was prepared to uphold the claim upon the ground either that the claim was a claim to such toll as may be reasonable from time to time: (and a toll may vary in amount from time to time. *Case of the Corporation of Maidenhead*, Palm. at p. 86) or upon the ground that within the time of legal memory the toll might have been reserved upon the dedication of the streets to the public.

But a prior case in the same volume of the Law Reports, *Bryant v. Foot*, L. R. 3 Q. B. 497, is an instance of an opposite conclusion. In that case it was proved that from the year 1808 to 1854 the fee paid on the celebration of a marriage in the parish church had been 13/- viz. 10/- to the rector and 3/- to the clerk. There was no evidence extending beyond 1808. The Court here having power to draw inferences of fact held that considering the difference in the value of money in 1189 and the present time, of which the Court will take judicial notice, it was impossible that a payment of 13/- on every marriage could have been made at that period, and that the objection of rankness applied, and rebutted the presumption, arising from uninterrupted modern usage, that the fee was taken as of right in the time of Richard I. It is to be observed that here the claim could not be upheld as a claim to a varying fee such as might be reasonable at the time since the Court was here prepared to hold that a marriage fee must be a fixed fee and cannot be of a varying amount.

So again in *Warrington v. Moseley*, 4 Mod. 319, a prescription for a toll of 2d. upon every pack of Manchester goods bought in Manchester except of the burgesses there was held bad. For without dealing with the other objections on the ground of uncertainty, viz. that the toll was on a *pack* which might be of varying size: though as to this it was answered that it was as certain as a prescription to have a halfpenny for every porter's burden laid upon Queenhithe to be conveyed thence by water which had been held good (Moor. fo. 825) though it was evident that one shore porter will carry more goods than another: the court was not satisfied with the prescription because there was no recompense for it, and every prescription to charge the subject with a duty, must import a benefit or recompense to him, or else some reason must be showed why a duty is claimed.

And as to the case in Dyer, 352 B., Trin. 18 Eliz. Anon. for Custom called Granage, where the Lord Mayor brought action on the case founded on a custom to have the 20th part of that salt of every stranger who brought it to the Port of London, which case was urged in argument, the Court considered it very hard without any reason being given for it. It certainly appears contrary to Magna Charta, cap. 30, which enacts "that all merchants may buy and sell without any manner of evil tolls."

An instance to the contrary of a toll allowed when there was a reason for it is found in *Ferrers's Case*, 1 Le. 108, pl. 147. There a claim to set up pens for sheep and to charge a toll for their use was held good being for a market which is for the common weal.

And in a case in the *Year Book*, 11 H. VI. 23, it was held that a man may prescribe to have a fair in the frank tenement of another. And also to assign booths there. Br. Ab., *Prescrip.* pl. 97.

Another case in which, curiously enough, salt was in question, where the prescription was held bad on the ground of uncertainty, and unreasonableness was *Prideaux v. Warne*, Raym. 232.

This case so far as reason is concerned seems to extend the requirement of service to the public, in order to support a charge, to the provision of everything requisite for the use of the port or market &c., in respect of which the charge is made.

There in replevin for taking a sail of a ship the defendant avows the taking for non-payment of a prescriptive bushel of salt due by every ship using a quay within his manor. The claim was held bad.

And Hale, C.J. said, " This prescription is only for a wharf, not for a port, and there ought to be reasonable recompense for the prescription : for Magna Charta says Omnes mercatores peregrinos &c., without unreasonable toll: and *he who hath a port ought to find and provide weights and measures* and other things."

The Law seems all along to have leant very strongly in favour of commerce, and in particular to the encouragement of markets. Thus in Br. Abr., *Customs*, pl. 48, citing *Y. B.* 12 E. IV. 8, it was held by the Court in an action of trespass, that where the defendant prescribed that in such a Vill had been a market such a day time out of mind, and justified for buying goods there, this was a good prescription, though it did not show to whom the market belongs, for per Littleton it goes with the land.

The Church was of course no less favoured than commerce. Thus a prescription to cut grass in another's land, to strew the Church is good, *Bond's Case*, 15 Car. So it will be remembered in *Gatewood's Case* it was said that Inhabitants, though not incorporated, may prescribe for a way to Church.

It has been held an unreasonable prescription to distrain for damage feasant and to retain the distress until a fine be paid at the will of the distrainor. For it is contrary to common right and reason that a man should be his own judge. Br. Abr., *Prescription*, pl. 101, Littleton, *Villeinage*.

So it is not a good prescription to have a heriot of every stranger dying within the manor, *Perkins v. Cumberford*, 41 El. B., Vin. Abr., *Prescrip.* 267.

If a man prescribes that if he finds goods within his manor that he shall have them, this is a void prescription; for it is contrary to reason, and a thing that cannot have a lawful commencement. Br. Abr., *Prescrip.* p. 93. *Doct. and Stud.*, lib. 2, c. 51.

So in *Y. B.* 42 E. III. 5 a prescription by a Sheriff to have a certain gift at every tourn was held unreasonable on the face of it, since a gift is at the will of the donor. To prescribe for a gift is really a contradiction in terms.

So where a Corporation prescribed to arrest a man for suspicion of felony and to imprison him for three days before sending him on to the next gaol, this was held unreasonable. *Y. B.* 22 E. IV. 43.

It is to be observed that a prescription for a free chase or warren is very much limited on this ground. No man can prescribe to have a chase or warren in any land but in his own demesnes, or in land within his fee and Seigniory. *Y. B.* 3 H. VI. 136.

This forms an interesting comment upon the theory of a grant underlying prescription. It shows that although in cases of prescription a grant was presumed, yet the presumption was only allowed to be made within certain limits, and those not so extensive as the possibilities of grant. Nothing that could not be granted could be prescribed for, but not everything that might be the subject of a grant could be gained by prescription. There can be no doubt that many a right may be granted that people generally, as represented by the ordinary common sense of a jury, would consider unreasonable; yet for that very reason no such right could be prescribed for.

Hence it was that a right of warren, though it could not originally be granted over the land of another, but might by assignment come to take effect over another's land, yet could not be prescribed for over the land of another. The lord may however prescribe for warren over all the lands within his fee and seigniory, because the tenants may well have received their grants originally subject to the warren.

Tolls again are a striking instance of how much more limited prescription is than grant. There can be no doubt that many of the tolls the prescription for which failed, might have been granted. So a right of prospect, though it can be granted, cannot be prescribed for. *Aldred's Case*, 9 Rep. 58. A.-G. on the Relation of *Gray's Inn v. Doughty*, 2 Ves. 453.

But with regard to prospect it must be borne in mind that it cannot be granted by *express agreement* so *as to create an easement annexed to the land*, but is created by covenant not to build or obstruct. This is of course binding in equity by notice, *Tulk v. Moxhay*, 2 Ph. 774. The action is brought on the covenant. (See as instances of numerous cases, *Manners v. Johnson*, 1 Ch. D. 673, *Western v. MacDermott*, 2 Ch. 72), and a recent case in the House of Lords, *Spicer v. Martin*, 14 App. Cas. 12. In *Samford and Havet's Case*, Godbolt, 184, in an action for trespass for 30 hares and 300 coneys hunted in his warren, taken and carried away, which trespass was laid with a continuance from such a time till such a time, Defendant justified because he had common in the place where, &c. to a messuage six yard lands for 240 sheep, and that he and those, &c. had used, time, &c. at such time as the common was surcharged with coneys to hunt them, kill and carry them as to his messuage appertaining. Plaintiff demurred, because a man cannot make such a prescription in the free warren and freehold of another: and secondly because a man cannot so prescribe to hunt kill and carry away his coneys as to his messuage pertaining: but he may prescribe to have so many coneys to spend in his house. And the prescription was held void. See too *The King v. Sherington Talbot*, Cro. C. 311.

There is a case quoted in *Y. B.* 43 E. III. 13 b. where the Lord of a Vill prescribed to have a warren in all the land within the Vill held of him, and it was argued that this was not good, for conies dig holes in the land and thus a man is deprived of the profit of his land. But that is not a good contention, because it does not deprive him of the whole profit of the land, which as we have seen, is the point at which a prescription is disallowed. See *Y. B.* 44 E. III. 12 b. But there can be no prescription for warren in lands not within the Seigniory, see *Y. B.* Hen. VI. 13 b.

Although it was not a good prescription to have a bushel of

salt from a ship that did not come up to the quay, yet it was decided in the case of *Crisp v. Bellwood*, 3 Lev. 424, that where Sir Willoughby Hickman was lord of the Manor of Gainsborough, within which was a wharf repaired by the Lord of the Manor; and the Lord prescribed to have a toll of 2*d.* a ton on all merchandises put on land within the Manor (not saying upon the wharf), this was a good prescription. It was also held good when the Corporation of Dublin prescribed that they are owners of the port and that they maintain perches in the said river and direct the ships in the deep channel, and that they maintain the quay and a crane ; and that in consideration of this they prescribe to receive of all merchandises in the said port 3*d.* of the pound. Mich. 6 Ja. I. in the Exchequer.

CHAPTER VI.

THE PUBLIC BENEFIT.

As might well be imagined, the public benefit is a consideration of importance in considering whether a prescription is to be allowed.

It is a clear rule that no prescription which is against the public good will be allowed.

Thus, in the *Count of Shrewsbury's Case*, adjudged in Hilary, 43 Eliz. in Queen's Bench, but cited only in the abridgements, it was held that if a man prescribes that he and his predecessors, who have been seised of the Manor of Coleherbert, have been exempt from the government of the Mayor of the City of London, and of all his officers, this is not a good prescription. For by this means they of that Liberty would be without government, which is against Law or public policy, and therefore void. It was further held that it is not a good prescription to claim that he and his ancestors, seised of the said Manor, have used to have Assise of bread and ale, and also to have the search of weights and measures, and to have the punishment of them: for this belongs properly to a Court Leet to punish, and he has not any court to punish such offences by presentment or otherwise.

So there can be no prescription to do a thing that is a public nuisance. 2 E. IV. 9.

So there can be no prescription to erect a gate across a public way, *James v. Hayward*, W. Jones, 222. And in *Dewell v. Sanders*, Cro. Jac. 591 a curious case was decided upon what was a nuisance. It was then held that the erection of a new pigeon-house by the freeholder of a manor is not a common nuisance; but if the pigeons fly abroad to the damage of the king's subjects the judges of Assise may take cognisance of it. See too *Prat v. Steam*, Cro. Jac. 382. The Court says "if it were a common nuisance neither the lord of the Manor nor the parson could erect a dovehouse more than any other freeholder; for none can prescribe to make a common nuisance, for it cannot have a lawful beginning by licence or otherwise, being an offence against the Common Law." So stern is the law against nuisances that even the licence of the king to make a nuisance is void. *Y. B.* 27 Ed. III. pl. 6. And *Y. B.* 22 Hen. VI. "if a man will plead a pardon for a nuisance, it is void as for the continuance thereof."

So again in *Fowler v. Sanders*, Cro. Jac. 446, it was held that a prescription to lay logs of wood for fuel in the highways before the doors of ancient houses, leaving sufficient room to pass, is bad, and though it is a public nuisance yet a person deriving any special damage may have a private action. A private nuisance may, however, be prescribed for. See among many cases *Goldsmid v. Tunbridge Wells Commrs.*, L. R. 1 Ch. 349, *Glossop v. Isleworth Local Board*, L. R. 12 Ch. D. 102.

So a man cannot prescribe to be discharged of his appearance at the Leet, by being sworn before the Constable and port-reeve.

Brooke, Abr., *Prescrip.* pl. 13. *Y. B.* 24 E. IV. 15. Nor is it a good prescription that the Lord of the Vill shall have fine of every tenant who marries his daughter without his licence. Brooke, Abr., *Prescrip.* pl. 101. Littleton, *Villeinage.* This affords a striking instance of how much more restricted the rights that can be gained by prescription are than those that might perfectly lawfully exist under the feudal tenures.

On the other hand, even wide claims which were for the public benefit might be gained by prescription, thus in *Abbot v. Weekly*, 1 Lev. 176, in trespass for breaking his close, the defendant prescribes that all the inhabitants of the Vill, time out of mind had used to dance there at all times of the year at their free will for their recreation, and so justifies. It was moved in arrest of judgment that this prescription to dance in the freehold of another and spoil his grass was void, especially as it is laid at all times of the year, and not at seasonable times. And that it was also ill as laid on the inhabitants, who, although they may prescribe in easements (*Gateward's Case*), yet they ought to be easements of necessity, as ways to a church, &c., and not for pleasure merely. But it was held a good prescription, for it is necessary for inhabitants to have their recreation, and that at all times of the year. But it may be asked how it can be reasonable or necessary to dance on grass at all times of the year. However, it must be observed that this was a decision after verdict, and the decision might well have been different upon demurrer.

So prescriptions for ways were always much favoured. Thus a man may prescribe to have a way over a churchyard, even though it be a sanctuary, 18 E. IV. 8, or even to have a way through a church, *ib.* Brook, *Abr.* Prescrip. pl. 91. And it was there said that the inhabitants of London had a prescriptive right of way through the churchyard of the Charterhouse.

CHAPTER VII.

PRESCRIPTION AGAINST DEFINITE RULES OF COMMON LAW, OR AGAINST STATUTES.

OF course it is difficult to say in some cases whether a prescription is bad as offending against a rule of Common Law, or against public policy. Indeed it may well be said that a due regard of public policy is one of the rules of the Common Law. However, there is a distinction more or less clear between those well-defined rules of Common Law, and of course express statutory exactments on the one hand, and the somewhat vague and general rule of the regard of public policy on the other.

Now, although it may seem rather paradoxical, yet such appears to be the fact, that a Court of Chancery, though its jurisdiction is in derogation of the Common Law, is itself in accordance with the Common Law. But since the jurisdiction is in derogation of the Common Law, a prescription will not lie to hold a Court of Chancery.

In *Martin v. Marshall and Key*, Hob. 63, the defendant prescribed for a Court of Chancery at York. It was agreed that a Court of Equity could not lie in grant, much less in prescription, being a jurisdiction to be derived from the Crown only. Meaning, I suppose, a jurisdiction inherent in and inseparable from the Royal prerogative. And so Hobart, C. J., in his report says it was resolved by Popham, Anderson, Gawdy and Walmsley, that the king could not grant to the queen to hold a Court of Equity.

This is certainly in accordance with the opinions of the judges given in the case of the Lords Presidents of Wales and York, to be found in XII. Co. 51. The Lords Presidents had objected to the issuing of prohibitions to them by the judges, restraining them from hearing causes. The judges go into the history of the institution of the Courts, showing how that in York was established in consequence of the insurrections of Lord Hussey, Sir Robert Ask and Sir Francis Bigot, quod pax et tranquillitas subditorum praeservetur. The judges say that any grant of a right to try real and personal actions by this commission would have been utterly void in law. For no such general authority granted may be made by the commission of the king to hear and determine all real actions within such a county according to law, as he may by Charter within a particular county or place. For the king by commission may give power to determine criminal causes between the king and the party, secundum legem et consuetudinem Angliae: but he cannot give power by commission to determine causes between party and party. *Scrogg's Case,* Dyer, 175 (though this report seems hardly wide enough for that). See too Dyer, 236.

But the king by his letters patent may grant to such a corporation in such a place, tenere placita realia, personalia et mixta, and none by this can have any prejudice, for the proceeding ought to be according to law; and if they err, the party grieved may have his writ of error; but the Crown cannot grant to them a Court of Equity for the cause aforesaid, and also for this cause that such a judge should be without controlment. And it was said that if such commissioners cannot determine felonies or other criminal causes by writ, but by commission, so cannot any determine private causes betwixt party and party by commission, but by writ by the Statute of Magna Charta, C. 12, and Statute West, 2 cap. 30. "Recognitiones de nova disseisina, &c. non capiantur nisi in propriis comitatibus:" which Act gives authority to justices of assise in their proper counties: by which it appears that without an Act of Parliament the king by his letters patent cannot put and authorise justices de assisis capiendis to take them within another county.

In *Martin v. Marshal,* Hobart, C. J., goes on to say that such a Court could not be granted (and therefore could not be prescribed for) for another reason, viz. that the king cannot grant anything in derogation of the Common Law. But tenere placita, according to the course of law, may be granted and prescribed for. As for the Chancery Courts of Chester and Durham, they are incidents of a County Palatine. It would seem therefore that a Chancery Court might indirectly be prescribed for as incidental to a County Palatine, which may be prescribed for. Co. Litt. 119 b.

As for the Courts of London and the Cinque Ports, they are by Act of Parliament.

He further says, " Indeed, I hold this to be a question of great consideration, that a Court of Equity should stand upon grant or prescription only. For though it be true that the Court of Chancery hath always been, and so in effect stands by a prescription, yet that is not well reasoned. For in pleading of anything done in Chancery you do not bring in your plea with a prescription as in these inferior pretended Courts, but you plead a thing done in the Court of Chancery as you do all things done in the Courts of Common Pleas or King's Bench. Whereof the reason is that they are fundamental Courts, as ancient as the kingdom itself (2 *Inst.* 23, Bracton 108, Mirror 8), and known to the law. For all kingdoms in their constitution are with the power of justice both according to the rule of law and of equity, both which being in the king as sovereign, were after settled in several Courts, as the light first being made by God was after settled in the great bodies of the Sun and the Moon. But that part of Equity being opposite to regular law, and in a manner an arbitrary disposition, is still administered by the king himself and his chancellor in his name ab initio, as a special trust committed to the king, and not by him to be committed to any other." See *Mayor of York's Case*, Godbolt, 262.

It appears that in London the mayor may prescribe to have a Court of Chancery of matters tried in the Sheriff's Court of London, though such court could not be granted by the letters patent of the king. *Andrew v. Webb*, Mich. 5 Jac. I. Vin. *Abr.* Pres. 266.

And so the Mayor's Court is called a Mark Court, because

it may mark any cause in the Sheriff's Court, even after verdict, but before judgment, and examine it. *ib.*

It seems that on the ground of conflict with the Common Law, the rule that a sheriff of a Court cannot prescribe for gifts, also void on the other ground of being a contradiction in terms, must be extended to cases when he would prescribe for fees. For he is a public officer so necessary for carrying on the government of the realm that he ought to take nothing for doing his office. *Y. B.* 42 E. III. 5.

The difference between what prescription is not allowed as being against the Common Law and what may stand as good is aptly illustrated by the case of Common of Fishery and the like.

Thus a man may prescribe to have separalem pischariam in such water, and thereby to exclude the lord of the soil (Co. Litt. 122), and the same to have separalem pischariam and exclude the owner of the soil either absolutely or from such a day to such a day, *ib.* See *North v. Cox,* I. Lev. 253; *Potter v. North,* I. Saund. 347; *Hopkins v. Robinson,* 2 Saund. 324.

And the same of sola vestura, Co. Litt. 4: 1b. 122, which does not exclude the lord from all the profits but leaves him the mines and the trees. But there can be no prescription to have common of pasture or estovers in the soil of another and exclude the owners—for this would be a prescription against the law—it would be repugnant to the meaning of common, which implies that the owner shall inter-common or as Coke puts it, 122 b. 'it was implied in the first grant that the owner of the soyle should take his reasonable profit there.' *White v. Shirland,* Pasch. 26 Eliz. K. B.

The same applies of course to common of pischary. *Chinery v. Fishen,* in C. B. Co. Litt. 122 b. and to every other right of common.

It seems however that when a common is claimed not repugnant by reason that divers several persons claim the common in respect of their tenements, yet it is also not repugnant on the ground that it claims to exclude the lord for a certain time, so long as the lord is not absolutely excluded, and is left his reasonable profit.

Thus in *Wheatland v. Paine*, Pasch. 12 Car. I. in B. R. The tenants of a manor prescribed to have the sole common for their horses in a meadow after the grass cut and made into cocks, by tying their horses there, so that they did not interfere with the grass, till Lammas Day; and after Lammas Day for all commonable beasts levant and couchant upon their tenements without tying or keeping in till Lady Day in Lent annually as to their tenements appertaining, excluding the lord of the meadow and manor from having any common or pasture there for this time, he having the soil of the meadow throughout the year and the whole herbage till Lammas or till the cutting, if he keeps it for hay. This was held a good prescription.

And it appears (despite the saying to the contrary in Vin. *Abr.* Pres. 269, 2) from the case of *Kenrick v. Pargiter*, Yelv. 129. That it would be a good prescription to claim common, and say that the lord ought not to put in more than his stint, for the lord may well be stinted. That case was decided in favour of the lord because the commoners had not gone on to claim a custom to distrain the lord's cattle damage feasant if he surcharged. And without the prescription his cattle could not be taken damage feasant in his own soil.

In *Dewclas v. Kendall*, Yelv. 187, or as it appears in Cro. Jac. 256, *Dowglasse v. Kendal*, in trespass for cutting thorns defendant prescribed to cut down and take away all the thorns growing in the said place to spend in his said house or about his lands, as appurtenant thereto. Plaintiff replied that Sir Richard Saltington was seised of the Manor of Chipping warden : that the thorns grew upon the waste of the said manor : and that he licensed the plaintiff to cut thorns. Defendant demurred, and it was found for the defendant. The court made a distinction between the case where a man claims reasonable estovers in another's soil and where he claims all the thorns in another's soil. In the first case, if the owner of the soil cuts the thorns first, he who has title of estovers cannot take them, for the property and interest of all the thorns continues in the owner of the soil and the other has but common there. And if the owner in such case cuts all the wood he who ought to have the estovers shall have an action on the case only, and not an assise : for when the whole is destroyed he cannot be put in seisin. But in this case defendants claim all the thorns ; and if they have all Sir R. Saltington can have none, and by consequence cannot license the plaintiff to cut any : and this is not a claim in the nature of estovers : for estovers are but parcel of the wood and that to be taken for a special purpose.

Now although the question what prescriptions are bad as contravening rules of public policy, or definite rules of the Common Law to the contrary, may appear somewhat vague and uncertain : we approach regions of greater precision when we come to consider prescriptions contrary to Statutes. Yet here at the outset of an apparently plain question, we are met by a difficulty arising out of the distinction taken between Statutes merely declarative of the Common Law and Statutes enacting some new prohibition.

What Coke says upon this subject is as follows : Co. Litt. 115a,

" This is the reason that regularly a man cannot prescribe or alledge a custom against a statute, because that is matter of record, and is the highest proofe and matter of record in law. But yet a man may prescribe against an Act of Parliament, when his prescription or custome is saved or preserved by another Act of Parliament.

" There is also a diversity betweene an Act of Parliament in the negative and in the affirmative : for an affirmative Act doth not take away a custome : as the Statute of Wills of 32 and 34 Hen. VIII. doth not take away a custome to devise lands, as it hath beene often adjudged. Moreover there is a diversity betweene statutes that be in the negative ; for if a statute in the negative be declarative of the ancient law, that is, in affirm-ance of the Common Law, there as well as a man may prescribe or alledge a custome against the Common Law, so a man may doe against such a statute : for as our author saith consuetudo, &c. privat communem legem. As the Statute of Magna Charta provideth that no leet shall be holden but twice in the yeare ; yet a man may prescribe to hold it oftener and at other times ; for that the statute was but in affirmance of the Common Law. (See 2 Hawk, *P. C.*, 56.)

"So the Statute of 34 Edw. I. provideth that none shall cut downe any trees of his own within a forest without the view of the forester; but inasmuch as this Act is in affirmance of the Common Law, a man may prescribe to cut down his trees within a forest without the view of the forester. And so it was adjudged in 16 Eliz. in the Exchequer by Sir E. Sanders, C.B., and other Barons of the Exchequer."

This seems an obviously sensible rule. If a Statute is merely declaratory of the Common Law, the law clearly remains the same : and any customs or prescriptions before allowable are not affected. But in considering whether any particular Statute is affirmative or negative what is to be looked at is the substantial effect of the Statute, and not the mere form. For a purely affirmative statute may well be expressed in negative terms. The negative words may arise from the nature of the subject, or be a mere mode of expression, and in such a case there can be no reason for giving a different effect to negative than to affirmative words. It would indeed involve a contradiction in terms, to say at the same time that a Statute though expressed in negative terms, is merely declaratory of the Common Law, and that it is introductive of new restrictions. The best way therefore of stating the rule seems to be as Coke himself elsewhere has it (2 *Inst.* 210), "a Statute made in the affirmative without any negative expressed or implied doth not take away the Common Law."

The instance given by Coke of Leets and Magna Charta does not seem the most fortunate that might have been chosen. Magna Charta provides Nec aliquis vicecomes vel ballivus, faciat turnum suum per hundredum, nisi bis in anno ; et nonnisi in loco consueto, videlicet semel post Pascha et iterum post festum sancti Michaelis : et visus de franco plegio tunc fiat ad illum terminum Sancti Michaelis sine occasione. But the case comes within the express exception made by Coke himself, when the Statute saves or preserves the custom or prescription. For it is expressly declared, Quod quilibet habeat libertates suas quas habuit et habere consuevit tempore Regis Henrici avi nostri vel quas postea perquisivit. See *Lawson and Hare's Case*, 2 Leon. 74. And of course the same objection would apply in another case when this very question of leets was discussed.   The case is also interesting for another part of the argument.

The Queen and Partridge's Case, 2 Leon. 28.   There in a quo warranto brought against Partridge it was holden by all the justices that a man might prescribe to hold a leet oftener than twice a year, and at other days than are set forth in Magna Charta (c. 35) because the said Statute is in the affirmative. But Popham, A. G., said that one cannot prescribe against a Statute.   And it was moved by him if a general pardon be granted with general exception in it, he which will have advantage of it ought to plead it and show that he is not any person excepted, for otherwise the judges cannot allow him the benefit of it, because they do not know if he be a person excepted or not.   But if there be special persons excepted by name then he need not to plead it, for the Court may discern J. D. from J. S. (8 E. IV. 7, 26 H. VIII. 7).   So if a man commits felony and also treason, and afterwards comes a general pardon for felony, but treason is excepted, and the party is arraigned for felony, by Coke he shall have the benefit of the pardon, Popham Contra, for he is disabled by the treason.   It was agreed by the whole Court that in a quo warranto it is not sufficient for the defendant to say that such a subject hath lawful interest to hold leets without making title to himself, for the writ is Quo Warranto he claims them.   And afterwards judgment was given for the queen.

There is also a certain difficulty about the other instance given by Coke, viz. that of cutting down trees in a forest without view of the forester.

The Statute mentioned by Coke, 34 E. I. appears to be only an ordinance and not a Statute.   But that is really immaterial since the same considerations will apply to the Charta de Foresta.   9 Hen. III. c. 4.

But it is contested that the negative in that Statute is of the kind stated by Coke, viz. merely one of form, the effect of the Statute being affirmative.   This opinion of Coke was noticed and contested by Noy, A. G., in *Lord Lovelace's Case* Sir W. Jones, 270.   He says, " There is a late opinion of Coke sur Litt. 115, that a prescription to fell and sell wood without view is good, yet it is clear that it is not, and so it was resolved 16 E. II. Rot. 53, in the Earl of Arundel's case."

Lord Richardson denied the difference taken by Coke as between negative Statutes declarative of the Common Law and negative Statutes introducing a new law; and he held against my Lord Coke, that in neither of those cases a prescription can be against a negative Statute. It seems clear however that in the general principle Coke is right and therefore less weight is due to a decision of a judge who disagreed with him upon that. The same question arose in the case of the *Tenants of the Manor of Bray*, Sir W. Jones, 289. In support of his contention about negative Statutes, Noy, A. G., quoted a case out of *Y. B.*[1] 20 H. VI. that though the Statute de Sylva Caedua be but in observance of the old law, viz. that no tythes ought to be paid of timber, yet that Statute being a negative a prescription to have timber is not good.

But Coke's instance reported to him by Popham is express. In Pickering, 8 E. III. Rot. 38, Henry de Reny Lord of the Manor of Leneor in the Forest of Pickering made a claim found by the foresters, verderours and regarders to be true, to have a woodward within the woods of his manor, and to cut, give away and sell the underwood without view of the foresters, and to kill foxes, hares, kids, &c. "Which claime by prescription the justices doubted only of two points. First, forasmuch as the said manor was within the limits of the forest it should not only be contra assisam forestae for his woodward to beare bow and arrowes where by law he ought to beare but an hatchet, and no bow nor arrows within the forest, but also de facili cedere possit in destructionem ferarum" &c., and they therefore doubted whether it might be claimed by prescription. The second doubt was of a similar kind not material. But of the other parts of the prescription no doubt at all was made; and the like had been allowed in the same eyre as in the case of Thomas Lord Wake of Lydell and of Gilbert of Acton, Rot. 37, and of others.

---

[1] This is a wrong reference; it should probably be 9 Hen. VI. 56, and in any case it is not a decision but only a query.

And the case of *Leicester Forest*, Cro. Jac. 155, seems clear to the same effect. The judges there all held that the owners of woods in a forest may cut them down at their pleasure without license or view of the foresters, but yet in such manner as they ought always to leave sufficient vert for the deer there. This however only extends to cutting down one's own wood.

But whether Coke is right or not in this instance, and he certainly seems to have the better authority with him, I think it is clear that his distinction is a good one, and founded upon the most obvious good reasoning. Further information upon these points is contained in the valuable notes to Coke upon Littleton in the 19th edition by Butler. If an instance be needed that there can be no prescription against a Statute distinctly negative there is one contained in Brook, *Abr.* prescrip. pl. 50, see 30, Ass. 38.

In trespass a defendant was condemned. He prescribed to distrain for rent upon the land held and to carry the distress to D in another county. And the Statute of Marlbridge, c. 4, provides that a man shall not distrain in one county and carry the distress into another county.

CHAPTER VIII.

PLEADING A PRESCRIPTION AGAINST A PRESCRIPTION.

IF a claim be made by prescription, no plea for a prescription entirely inconsistent with it is good of itself. The prescription in the declaration must be traversed, and then the prescription in the plea may stand. *Murgatroid v. Law*, Carth. 117. *Aldred's Case*, 9 Rep. 58 b., also is clear upon the point, adopting as it does the conclusion of a prior case of *Hickman v. Thorney*, Godb. 183. In the report in Coke, Wray, C. J., and the whole Court say, "(1) When a man has a lawful easement or profit by prescription from time whereof &c , another custom which is also from time whereof &c., cannot take it away; for the one custom is as ancient as the other: as if one has a way over the land of A to his freehold by prescription from time whereof &c., A cannot alledge a prescription or custom to stop the said way, and (2) it may be that before time of memory the owner of the said piece of land has granted to the owner of said house to have the said windows without any stopping of them and so the prescription may have a lawful beginning." (See 1 Roll. *Abr.* 566). Of course it is true that these cases and the rules they establish are really only of importance historically, as showing how pleas were required to be framed in the old days of strict and technical pleading. And pleading in the matter now must of course be according to the rules under the Judicature Acts: but it is not quite easy to see how far some of these old cases may be of importance in any case arising under the new rules. However that is of less importance now because prescriptive claims nowadays are mostly of the class dealt with by the prescription Act, and turn for the most part upon that Act.

Now *Russell and Broker's Case*, 2 Leon. 209, is an interesting one upon the point.

There Russell brought trespass against Broker for cutting down of four oaks. The defendant prescribed for reasonable estovers, and the plaintiff replied the forest law requiring view of the forester. The defendant demurred. And the Court found for the defendant; on two grounds, he ought to have specially pleaded the Forest Law and not merely alleged it. Or otherwise the plaintiff ought to have traversed the prescription of the defendant. "For here are two prescriptions, one pleaded by the defendant by way of bar: the other set forth by the plaintiff in his replication without any traverse of that which is alleged in the bar, which can be good. But if the plaintiff had shewed in his replication Lex forestae talis est &c., then the prescription of the defendant had been answered without more, for none can prescribe against a Statute." See *Spooner v. Day*, Cro. Car., 432, where the plaintiff prescribed for a fold course. The defendant pleaded in bar a custom to inclose, but without any difficulty it was adjudged that the bar was not good: because it did not traverse the prescription in the declaration. "And he cannot plead a prescription against prescription but he ought to answer the prescription alledged in the Court."

As to the distinction between a fold course and a frank foldage, see Williams *on Commons*, p. 277.

In *Sharp v. Bechenowe*, Lutwyche, p. 398, it is said "foldage is a liberty to have another man's sheep folded on my land, and a fold course is to have pasture for a certain number of my own sheep upon another man's land."

But a prescription or custom may be pleaded in answer to another without a traverse, where the latter is not inconsistent with but merely a qualification of the former. See 1 Chitty Pleading (4th edit.) p. 537. The true rule seems to be well put in a note in 1 Blackst. 49. He says, "whenever any material fact is alleged in any pleading which will, upon issue joined, decide the cause one way or other, if the adverse party plead a matter inconsistent with and contrary to such allegation, he must traverse it. But where a material point alleged by one party is fully confessed and avoided, that is, where the other party sets up a matter consistent with such allegation, but which, if true, is an answer to it, there he cannot also traverse it."

The authorities are collected and the points discussed in Sergeant Williams' note to *Bennett v. Filkens*, 1 Wms. Saund. 22 a.

In *Kinchin v. Knight*, 1 Blackst. 48, in trespass for rooting up his soil by turning hogs upon his land, defendant prescribes for right of common for hogs. Plaintiff replies by allowing the right, but qualifies it by insisting, that by another custom the swine ought to be rung. Defendant demurs, and argues that the replication is bad because two contrary customs cannot be pleaded but the first custom must be traversed. But the Court held that one custom or prescription may be pleaded against another where both may stand together. And these two customs may stand together, being consistent with each other: the one being only a regulation of the other. But there seems to be some difficulty in deciding when the second custom is consistent with the first and merely a modification of it, and when it is directly contrary. Thus in *Parkin v. Radcliffe*, 1 Bos. and Bul. 282. A lord of a manor prescribed upon the admission of a new tenant to have an heriot of the best chattel or best beast. Defendant pleaded " that on the said manor there had been from time whereof etc., a certain other ancient and laudable custom used and approved within the same, that is to say, that at the Court Baron of the lord of the said manor for the time being held in and for the said manor the homage of the said Court Baron had time whereof etc., been used to assess upon their oaths a reasonable sum of money to be paid upon the admission of every customary tenant, after such admission in lieu of a heriot by the said custom."

Upon this Eyre, C. J., says, " My difficulty is how to incorporate the two customs. The landlord pleads a custom to have the best live or dead chattel as a heriot. The tenant answers that he is not entitled to the best live or dead chattel but to a sum of money by way of compensation. This is pleaded two ways, (1) as a sum of money to be assessed absolutely by the homage, (2) as a sum to be agreed upon by the lord and the tenant, and on failure of an agreement then to be assessed by the homage. Either of those pleas is an absolute denial of the custom that the lord should have the best live or dead chattel. This compensation is pleaded to be in lieu of a heriot ; but since it is stated not to depend upon the will either of lord or tenant, but to take place in all cases it cannot be in lieu, it ought therefore to have been stated in the name of a heriot and as an inducement to a traverse.

"If the plaintiff had said, True, there is such a custom but if the tenant prefer to pay a sum of money in lieu, then he shall pay such sum as the parties shall agree upon, that would have been a modification of the custom, and the money would have come in lieu of the original right of the landlord, but here the original right is stated in two contradictory ways."

In *Hickman v. Thorney*, Freem. 209, the Court seem to have some vague notion that in some cases a prescription might be pleaded against a prescription, but did not seem exactly to know what they were, or what was the ground for them.

In that case the plaintiff prescribed for common. The defendant rejoined that there was a custom in the said field that any owner of lands might enclose any parcel of land lying together in the said field, and exclude the commoners in the said field. The plaintiff demurred that this was a prescription against a prescription without traversing the first. But the Court seemed to incline that it may be well enough, "for a particular prescription may be controlled by a general custom, though it cannot by another prescription : as in the case where a man prescribes for a way or for lights, another cannot prescribe to stop them up : for when they were once stopped up there is an end of them. But here is a custom that is of greater latitude and extent than the prescription, so it may be good without traversing the prescription, for if one or two men inclose, yet the party has his common in the residue, and so it may stand with prescription."

This last sentence seems to be the right reason, it makes the case square with the other cases quoted and the rule to be derived from them. This would be a case where the counter prescription is consistent with that in the declaration, but is merely a modification of it. In the report of the same case in 2 Mod. 79, it is stated that Atkyns, J., much doubted of the case at bar because the defendant had pleaded the custom to inclose in bar to a freeholder, who had no land in the common field where he claimed right of common. See *Hughes v. Keen's Case*, Godb. 183.

CHAPTER IX.

How the Prescription must be pleaded.

The first point to notice in this connection is that a prescription ought to be made in the affirmative, and not in the negative. Many a prescriptive right that might have been established was lost by reason that it was not properly alleged in the pleadings. It will be observed that this rule against a prescription in the negative excludes limitation, which is always in the negative, from all claim to be considered prescription at all.

The rule is well established and is to be found in the early Year Books.

Thus in the *Y. B.* 11 Ed. IV. 2 b., in the case before alluded to, of a prescription by the sergeants to be impleaded by writ original and not by bill, the objection was taken that this was a prescription in the negative and was therefore bad. It was agreed and held by the Court that in a mere negative a man cannot prescribe, but that he may well prescribe in a pregnant negative, or a negative mixed with an affirmative. This prescription was therefore a good one, as it was a claim to be impleaded by writ original, and was not vitiated by the mere addition of the negative part, not to be impleaded by bill. The substance of the claim was an assertion of an affirmative right.

So again *Y. B.* 8 Ed. IV. 5. Darley and all his companions agreed that if a man prescribes he must do so in the affirmative and not in the negative. The case is also useful as being very clear upon the point that there is no necessity to prescribe for a thing that one may do of common right. But the rule thus broadly stated may be rather misleading. It is true no doubt that a prescription in the affirmative is not harmed by the addition of a negative to define its limits, when the claim is in substance an affirmative one ; and it may well be that it would be bad in form if it were pleaded in the negative. But the dictum would apparently support the converse proposition that a prescription essentially negative which would clearly be bad if alleged negatively, can be made good by being turned round and presented in an affirmative form. To hold this would be to make the distinction an entirely nugatory one except for the purpose of the pettiest technicality. What is meant by the dictum I conceive to be this. That the claim, e.g., to be quit of toll, is in substance an affirmative one, which may be good if pleaded properly. The claim would be one to have done or paid something to be quit of toll. And even if this was allowed to stand without alleging the consideration, which might be allowed to be presumed upon proof of the usage from time of memory, yet the claim would be in substance not a mere negative plea of a statute of limitation, but an affirmative claim.

What has to be considered is, first, is the claim in substance affirmative ? If it is not, it cannot succeed though pleaded affirmatively. If it is, then it can only succeed if pleaded in the affirmative. If this is borne in mind I think it will be found that the rule is established not only in precedent, but in good sense.

It will be remembered that in the case of Tithes, quite apart apparently from any question of pleading, there can be no prescription in non decimando. *Slade v. Drake,* Hob. 297.

The view that a prescription to go quit of toll is in substance an affirmative claim, and not a pure negative, masquerading in an affirmative garb, is supported by Brook, *Ab.* Pres. pl. 17. He there says that a man must not prescribe not to pay toll, but to buy and sell quite freely, and therefore not to pay any toll. This would be a prescription quite on all fours with that of the Serjeant, to be impleaded by writ and not by bill, which is good.

This is brought out still more plainly in *Y. B.* 8 H. VI. 4, where a return to a writ had been quod a tempore, &c., non debuit nec consuevit aliquis abstrahi, &c., per breve de nativo habendo. It was there said that this was not a good custom "for it is in the negative, and not at all like the case that has been put of being quit of toll: for that is (really) in the affirmative, viz., that he and his ancestors whose estate he has in the same manor, have been used to buy in such a market, or such a fair from time, &c., and to pay nothing for toll: so that at all events this custom is laid in the affirmative, that they have been used to buy, coupled be it with a negative, to pay no toll. For it is no good custom to show that he has paid no toll from time of memory. For neither he nor any of those whose estate he has in the manor may ever have bought anything in the market, and there would then have been no advantage in the quittance. So in every custom there must be an affirmative, to show that the thing has been put in use."

This puts the objection to a pure negative on real solid ground. It might well be true of the person pleading the prescription that he had never paid any toll, but it was equally true of people generally: and for the same reason: that they might never have required to use the market, so that a pure negative, even if proved, did not amount to an assertion of title to the right claimed.

The instance given in Brook, *Ab.* Pres. pl. 65, of the prescription in the Cinque Ports, that the writ of the king does not run there, which is held to be a good prescription, though certainly negative in form, may be explained in the same way. It is really an affirmative—that the warden has jurisdiction in the Cinque Ports, with a negative—that the king's writ does not run there. The negative is thus a mere addition to and definition of the affirmative, which is the real substance of the claim. It is really an instance of the same kind as the case in which it is quoted, the case of the Sanctuary of Westminster in *Y. B.* 2 Edw. IV. 18. There the prescription was that there was the Sanctuary, and that all actions of debt, trespass or other contracts made therein were wont to be tried there before the commissioners and *in no other place.* A clear affirmative with a negative, see too *Y. B.* 22 H. VI. 14, where a prescription by the Prior of St. Nedeport that he had three mills there, and no one else had a mill, was apparently held good. Though it is to be observed that in this case the negative is not so clearly merely a limitation of the affirmative, but is apparently a separate prohibition. However if, as no doubt was the case, the object of the prescription was to compel all the people in the place to bring their corn to be ground at the mills of the prior, then the negative part would be a necessary adjunct of the affirmative and the only way of making it effective. So that this case also would be no extension of the rule, and would be quite consistent with the cases already cited.

This is perhaps the most important of the rules of pleading with reference to prescription. But there are a number of others to be gathered from decided cases which it will be necessary to notice.

In a prescription upon a presentment in *Y. B.* 21 Edw. IV. 38, it was laid that such an one ratione tenurae of right ought to repair a road between D. and S. It was moved that this prescription was bad since it ought to have alleged that he and all those whose estate he has &c. But the whole Court was of opinion that it was good in as much as it was stated to be by reason of tenure, which implies a title of prescription. It seems that in early times the rule of pleading was different as against the owner of the soil, and against a mere wrongdoer, where it was sufficient to declare generally on the possession. See *Strode v. Byrt,* 4 Mod. 420; *Kenrick v. Taylor,* 1 Wils. 326; *Waring v. Griffith,* 1 Burr. 443.

But this rule, when a liability is charged, seems to have afterwards been the same in both cases. See *Blockley v. Slater,* 1 Lutw. 119. *Sands v. Trefuses,* Cro. Car. 575. *Chapman v. Flexman,* 2 Ventr. 291.

And the true rule of pleading is laid down by Buller, J., in *Rider v. Smith,* 3 T.R. 766, " the distinction is between cases where the plaintiff lays a charge upon the right of the defendant, and where the defendant himself prescribes in right of his own estate. In the former case, the plaintiff is presumed to be ignorant of the defendant's estate, and cannot therefore plead it, but in the latter the defendant, knowing his own estate in right of which he claims a privilege, must set it forth. And notwithstanding two out of the three judges were of a different opinion in *Holback v. Warner,* Cro. Jac. 665, yet several subsequent cases have been determined on the above distinction. See *Tenant v. Goldwin,* Salk. 360. *Winford v. Woollaston,* 3 Lev. 266, and 1 Ventris Anon.

In the above case in *Y. B.* 21 Ed. IV. 38, it was argued that it ought not to be good merely to allege that he and his ancestors had used. It was agreed that that was bad, but for the reason that a man cannot be charged by the act of his ancestors without profit to be taken by it. Though in the case of an abbot this does not hold good. In such a case it is good to say that the Abbot of W. and all his predecessors have used, without any tenure, by reason that the mystical body of the abbacy never dies, but the office of the house continues to the successors in fee.

Of course declarations and pleas of prescription were, as all other pleas and declarations, subject to the technical rule against duplicity.

It would be starting upon an enquiry, interesting no doubt and instructive, but not legitimately within the scope of the present subject, if I were to attempt to expound, even in a cursory manner, all the highly technical rules of pleading that obtained in our Courts prior to recent changes.

A good deal of time and ingenuity might be spent in dealing exhaustively with the single rule against duplicity. That I do not intend to do. But it has an important bearing upon some cases of interest, and my task would not be complete without some reference to it. I do not think I can treat the subject more concisely than by quoting some part of the explanation given in Chitty *on Pleading,* 7th edit., Vol. 1, pp. 249 seq. 559. He says, "the object of the science of pleading is the production of a single issue upon the same subject-matter of dispute. The rule relating to duplicity or doubleness, tends more than any other to the attainment of the object. It precludes the parties, as well the plaintiff as the defendant, in each of their pleadings from stating or relying upon more than one matter constituting a sufficient ground of action, in respect of

the same demand, or a sufficient defence to the same claim, or
an adequate answer to the precedent pleading of the opponent.
The plaintiff cannot by the Common Law rule, in order to sustain
a single demand, rely upon two or more distinct grounds or
matters, each of which, independently of the other, amounts to
a good cause of action in respect of such demand. Thus at
Common Law, in a declaration upon a bond, the plaintiff could not
assign two breaches of the condition, because the bond was forfeited by one breach, which was sufficient to support his action,
though in covenant several breaches of different covenants
might be stated. And the same count must not contain two
promises in respect of the same subject-matter, as a promise to
pay a specific sum for a horse, and also a promise to pay for the
same horse, as much as it is worth."

(P. 558), "Every plea must in general be single, and if it
contain two distinct matters either of which would bar the
action, and each of which requires a separate answer, it will
in general be subject to a special demurrer for duplicity. Thus
if several outlawries be pleaded in the same plea to the same
matter, or if son assault demesne and a release be relied upon
in one plea to the same trespass, as either of these would defeat the action, the plea would be considered double. But the
defendant is not precluded from introducing several facts into
one plea, if they be constituent parts of the same entire defence, and form one connected proposition, or be alleged as
inducement to, or as a consequence of, another fact. Thus in
detinue at the suit of a feme, the defendant pleaded that after
bailment of the goods to him by the plaintiff she married
E. F., and that during such marriage E. F. released to him
all actions. It was objected that the plea was double, viz.
property in the husband by the marriage, and a release by
him. But it was resolved not to be double because he could
not plead the release without showing the marriage. So it
will be no duplicity to set out several matters, as a will or
deed and a fine constituting a title: although one of these
matters would defeat the action." He amplifies the subject
much more in various parts of his treatise, but this will, I
think, be sufficient for my purpose.

Now, in an assise for common appendant it is sufficient to claim the common as appendant, for that includes and implies a prescription. So held by Newton and all the Court in *Y. B.* 22 H. VI. 10.

And further, a plea of appendancy and prescription is bad for duplicity: that is, if the plea is first as common appendant, and then a prescription. But it seems that to claim common appendant alone, or to prescribe for common appendant is not double, for in the latter case it is only prescription that is in issue.

Thus in *Y. B.* 11 H. VI. 11, in trespass for cutting underwood, the defendants pleaded that each of them was seised of a house and a certain quantity of land in the town of B, and they and their ancestors and all those whose estate they had in the said land and tenements from time, &c. had a profit à prendre in a waste which contained 8 acres of land called T, to cut underwood to burn in their said houses and to repair their houses, &c. It was objected that this was a double plea of appendancy and prescription. But the Court held that, though it was a claim of profit as appendant, yet it was only claimed by prescription, and therefore was not a double plea. Though the Court agreed that the case put by the counsel for the plaintiff, viz. if the defendants in trespass were to say that he was seised of a house by reason of which he had common appendant, and that he and his ancestors, &c., putting in a plea of prescription, would have been a double plea. But where there is only one issue of the prescription, the plea is not double. See *Y. B.* 21 Edw. III. 40, 4 H. VI. 13: Br. *Ab.* Pres. pl. 96, ib. pl. 87. So in *Y. B.* 39 H. VI. 29. In a writ of Mesne brought by an abbot against one Elis, the count was that land was held of the defendant by the plaintiff, the abbot, in frankalmoign, and that the defendant and his ancestors, whose heir he was, had acquitted the plaintiff and his predecessors time out of mind, &c., and issue was taken upon the prescription. It was objected that the count was double— the frankalmoign and the acquittal—either of which was a sufficient defence. But it was held not to be double: either on the ground, as suggested by Choke, that the issue was taken upon the prescription, and that one ground was relied upon so as to avoid the doubleness: or, as suggested by Prisot, that though frankalmoign is generally a sufficient ground for acquittal, yet that is only so when it is pleaded so as to be a good ground: and here it is not so pleaded as the deed of grant in frankalmoign is not shown. And a gift in frankalmoign has never been held good without showing the deed.

A good instance of two prescriptions being held not to be bad for duplicity, upon the ground that they were both necessary for the one issue, is to be found in *Crouch v. Fryer*, Cro. Eliz. 784; Yelv. 2. However, in the report in Croke there is not the double prescription: there is the mere claim to be copyholder.

In Yelverton's report, however, it does appear. In that case, although there was a prescription upon a prescription, one in the copyholder to make his estate good, the other in the bishop to make his discharge good, yet it was allowed. " For a prescription in the lord, ought of necessity in common intendment to precede the prescription in the estate of the copyholder, and the discharge of the tithes in the lord (which may well be in this case because he is a spiritual person) shall trench to the benefit of the tenant who is the copyholder. For by this means it is presumed that the lord has the greater fines and rents.

" Nota, Popham was against this judgment because the plaintiff, who is the copyholder, will have *in suo genere* an estate of inheritance distinct from the estate of the lord, who is the bishop."

In a case in *Y. B.* 19 H. VI. 75, a nice technical point arose upon a count in prescription. There in a writ of annuity a plaintiff counted by prescription. The defendant showed that it began by composition. But the Court held that it would stand. For as Newton, J., said, "If he counts on the composition, then the composition will come in issue. And if the composition was made before time of memory, that cannot be tried, so that the prescription will come in issue. While if the title had its beginning with the possession after time of memory, that will be a question for the jury, and if they cannot find the beginning, then the prescription is good."

There are several points to be noted with regard to assises of rent.

In an assise of rent, if a man prescribes in him and his ancestors and in those whose estate he has, he ought to show deed of the rent: since there cannot be the que estate of the rent without deed. So that if a man shows deed of grant of the rent to his ancestor, but does not show deed of commencement of the rent, that is not sufficient. For though a man may prescribe in him and his ancestors, &c. without showing deed, yet he cannot prescribe in a que estate of a thing which cannot be granted without deed, without showing the deed creating it.

But the opposite is true of an acquittal in him and those whose estate the lord has in the seigniory of common appendant or estovers or other profits appendant. In such cases prescription may be without showing the deed of commencement of the acquittal. Br. *Ab.* Prescrip. pl. 29.

But he may prescribe in rent parcel of or appendant to a manor without showing specialty. Br. *Ab.* Pres. pl. 47. See Br. *Ab.* Monstrans, pl. 91.

The same applies to rent reserved for equality of partition. The reason in all these cases is that as the manor or land may pass by livery without deed, no deed is necessary to create the que estate. However, in 23 Ass. 6, occurs a case where Wilby, J., held, and was affirmed in error by Shard, J., that, in an assise of novel disseisin of rent a good title by prescription was made out without producing the deed creating it, or showing otherwise how his ancestors got it: so long as he could prove that he and his ancestors had been seised from time of memory. This certainly seems to be in accord with the principle upon which the Courts acted in case of other prescriptions, viz. presuming that when the thing might have had a lawful beginning, the commencement was in fact lawful.

But the same rule appears to have been followed in the case of a hundred. For it was held by Hill that a man cannot

prescribe in him and his predecessors and those whose estate
he has in a hundred without showing deed of the que estate,
Br. *Ab.* Pres. pl. 15. And it has been held that in an assise
of rent a man may not say that he and all those whose estate
he has in a messuage have had 20*s.* rent issuing out of the land
of the defendant, time out of mind, if he does not claim such as
appendant to the messuage. Br. *Ab.* Pres. pl. 26.

But it has been held that, at any rate in an action for
disturbance of common against a wrong doer, it is not necessary for the plaintiff to show title to the common. It is
sufficient if he says he is seised of a house, and de jure de-
buisset habere communiam. This is then sufficient for a
claim by prescription. *Strode v. Byrt*, 4 Mod. 420. The
Court says, "It is true if it had been upon special pleading,
as in trespass for distraining of his cattle, and the defendant
had pleaded that he was owner of the soil, and so justified
the taking, the plaintiff must have replied and showed a title
either by grant or prescription or some other conveyance."

If a man prescribes to have rent and distrain for it, it
is no plea that the rent has at all times been paid under
coercion, viz. of the distress: because the rent has been paid
time out of mind, and therefore though it began in tort it is
good, so as not to be avoided by the fact of having always
been paid under coercion. So held by all the justices. Br.
Ab. Pres. pl. 75.

But in prescribing for rent, and to distrain for it, care
must be taken to prescribe for the rent, and not merely for
the remedy by distress. For in *Stephens v. Lewis*, Cro. Eliz.
673, a prescription was laid that J. S., who was the owner of
the rent, was seised in fee, and that he and all his ancestors
had used to distrain for that rent in the said land; prescribing in the distress only and not in the rent. And
Anderson and Glanville held clearly that the prescription
ought to have been in the rent: and they said the law was
clear. But Williams, Serjeant, cited a case as having been
ruled in 14 Eliz. to the effect that a prescription alleged on
the distress was good. Of course it is easy to see that there
may not have been such uniformity of decision in earlier stages

of our judicial administration as at the present day, when there
are Courts of Appeal continually sitting, and it is not a matter
of great moment to present an appeal. So that in considering
the law in early times, it may well be that the opinion of my
Lord Brooke in his abridgement should be followed rather than
a stray case to the contrary in the year books, where that occurs
and cannot be reconciled.

Now it is to be observed that in a claim of rent it is
good to say that the plaintiff and all those seised of the
manor of D have been seised of the rent time out of mind
as parcel of the Manor. *Y. B.* 12 H. IV. 8, pl. 13 Br. *Ab.*
Pres. pl. 16, Per Hull, quod Hankford concessit. So again in
replevin a man prescribed for common, and that the defendant
and his ancestors had used to pay 10*s.* rent per annum to him
and his ancestors for the same common, and so avowed for
10*s.* And this was held good, notwithstanding that he did
not prescribe that he and his ancestors, &c. have had the
rent, but prescribed that the other has paid it; for it really
amounts to the same thing: and notwithstanding also that he
had prescribed for it as rent, whereas it was not rent, but
annuity, as it issued out of his own land.

In this connexion of a prescription to distrain there are
one or two more points worthy of notice. It was always necessary in every prescription to set out exactly what the right
was that was claimed. Thus if one claimed rent by prescription and wished to distrain for it, one ought also to prescribe
in the distress.

This general principle has appeared in many of the cases
already noticed, and is clearly laid down by Holt, C. J., in *The
King v. Speed,* 12 Mod. 329. The question there was whether
a process to levy a distress upon the goods of a man convicted
of deer-stalking was regular. In his judgment Chief Justice
Holt says:

" When one entitles himself to a duty and remedy by prescription, he must set out his remedy wholly. Indeed, if you
prescribe to a duty, you may have debt for it without prescription, but you cannot distrain without it; and if you prescribe to
duty and distress, you cannot, by virtue thereof, sell without a

prescription for selling too, because a prescription may be to distrain without selling."

Of course in pursuance of this general principle one is only bound to clearly claim those remedies which may or may not be attached to the right claimed. Anything that is merely and necessarily incidental to the right or the remedy need not be specified.

An instance of this, though not a very good one, since it really turned rather upon another point, is to be found in *Y. B.* 15 E. IV. 29, where Littleton gives a case that a sheriff prescribed in 5*s.* rent in such a vill for all sheriffs, etc. and it was held bad; for he is only as a tenant at will. By which he prescribed that it has been used time out of mind as above, and that they have used to distrain for it. This was held good. The principal case there too is a prescription or claim of usage by the inhabitants of Coventry. As to the sheriff's claim it is said Vin. *Abr.* Presc. 287, in a marginal note, that the prescription will run " that the king and his progenitors have had time out of mind 5*s.* of the vill etc. to the use of him who shall be sheriff for the time."

An excellent instance of how a claim should be pleaded is to be found in *John Joyce's Case*, Godb. 55, where a great many points of pleading were raised.

The fourth error assigned was that the claim being for scouring a gutter between the two messuages it ought to have said that the defendant's house was contigue adjacens to the plaintiff's house. And a case was cited from *Y. B.* 22 H. VI. when cattle had escaped into the plaintiff's close, and in an action of trespass the defendant had pleaded that it was by reason that the plaintiff had not fenced his field. But the plea was held bad because it did not allege that the plaintiff's close was adjacens.

The second error assigned was the uncertainty in claiming for all tenants.

That point is well exemplified in *Grymes v. Peacock*, 1 Bulst. 17. There is an action of trespass for taking turf and stones in the waste of the plaintiff, who was lord of the manor, the defendant justified by an usitatum fuit that it had been there used that every tenant for years of an ancient tenement within the said manor used to have common of turbary and of lymestones in the waste of the said manor, and so on, setting out the facts which were found by the jury.

But it was held that though the common was appurtenant to the messuage and close, yet the lessee could not have it by the prescription: for an usage ought to be perpetual, which could not be the case here, since it was interrupted by every new lease. Also a lessee for years cannot have right of common by prescription because the commencement and determination of his estate is certain, so that no usage can be alleged of it. And so of tenants at will in *Y. B.* 9 H. VI. 62.

It was there held that a lord cannot prescribe for himself and his tenants at will, because the tenants at will cannot prescribe; but his prescription should be that he and his predecessors, or his ancestors, or those whose estate he hath, have used for themselves and their tenants at will. The same may be said of *Cornelius v. Taylor*, Sid. 237, which shows that point, and also affords a striking instance of how precise the allegation was required to be. There in trespass quare clausum fregit in C. the defendant pleaded that the Manor of C. was an ancient manor, and that within the said manor was a custom that every tenant should have a way over the said place. The plaintiff demurred, and the plea was held bad: not on the ground that he claimed as tenant, for here he was claiming by a custom within the manor, which is good for every kind of tenant, as has already been shown ; see too *Pearce v. Bacon*, Cro. Eliz. 390.

But (1) because it was not alleged that the place where the right was claimed was within the manor, and therefore the custom would not extend to that. If the place were outside the Manor it would have been necessary for the tenant to prescribe in the name of the Lord.

And (2) because the claim had been that every tenant haberet, and not that all the tenants usi fuerunt habere, so that it was bad as not being a direct affirmation.

But in Viner's *Abridgment*, Pres. 291, a declaration that he and all, &c. *by himself or servants* had fetched water was held well enough as being a claim for him and his predecessors, for themselves and their servants, laying no prescription on the servants.

Again, *Underwood v. Saunders*, 2 Lev. 178, shows that if a claim is made for tenants without specifying of what kind, that would include all kinds and so be bad.

There are some cases that show the importance of laying the prescription as attached to something of a continuing nature where a prescription pure was in question. Of course where it is an allegation of a custom, as by copyholders of a custom within the manor, the custom itself has to stand for the continuance. See Co. Litt. 113 b. In *Matches v. Broughton*, Freem. 357, in an action upon the case the plaintiff counted that whereas betwixt his house and the defendant's there was a little piece of ground, called a twitchill, upon which he and all those whose estate he had, had used to set their ladders to repair their house, and said that he was possessionatus of the said house, &c., and that defendant erected a wall there per quod he could not set his ladder. It was held bad, for he had laid the prescription in himself and those whose estate he had, and said that he was possessionatus, which could only apply to a particular estate, as on lease for years, and a lessee ought not to prescribe in his own name. Rainsford said if he had said seisitus it might have been well enough. But Wylde held that it must have been seisitus in feodo, or else it might have been only an estate for life; but that if he had laid it in the occupiers perhaps it might have been good, being but an easement. But see as to the difference in relying on the possession in a declaration and a plea, *Grinstead v. Marlowe*, 4 T. R. 719; *Coryton v. Lithebye*, 2 Saund, 113 note.

But the case of *Scoble v. Skelton*, 2 Mod. 311, is express upon this point, that the declaration must be of a seisin in fee.

Now a claim by prescription rested upon usage time out of mind: therefore usage time out of mind was a necessary part of the claim.

Thus in *Goodwin v. Brooks*, T. Jones, 227, in trespass for taking and carrying away the plaintiff's cheeses, the defendant justified that he was seised in fee of Chipping Sudbury, and of an ancient market there every Thursday, and that he and all those whose estate he had, had used to have a penny for every hundred cheeses exposed to sale in the market by name of the Pitching Penny, and on denial to distrain.   And for the said penny for one hundred of cheeses being exposed there to sale being demanded and not paid, he distrained.   On demurrer an objection was taken that the defendant had not made a sufficient title, not having alleged usage time out of mind, but only by those whose estate he had.   And of this opinion was the whole Court.   So that judgment was given for the plaintiff.

The like was held in a prescription for common of vicinage, the essence of which is usage time out of mind, *Jenkins's Case*, Latch. 161.

Rolls argued that it was sufficient to claim without alleging time out of mind because that was necessarily implied.   He quoted a case in *Y. B.* 21 H. VII. 35, where in pleading a public right of way it was held not necessary to allege that it had been so time out of mind.   But Doderidge, Jones and Whitlock, held it ill, because in this case the usage time out of mind is the ground of the right of common of vicinage.   But they said that in a claim for common appendant the case is different, because in such a case an allegation of usage time out of mind would introduce doubt (? would be bad for duplicity; see Brook, *Ab.* double plea, 115), common appendant implying the usage time out of mind, Brook, *Ab.* Pres. pl. 23 ; *Y. B.* 22 H. VI. 10.

The true rule as to the necessity of alleging usage time out of mind is discoverable when one considers whether the claim is one in accordance with common right, as common appendant, which was a right belonging by the Common Law to the tenants of the manor, or was in accordance with common right by reason of rendering some service to the public, as e.g. carrying letters, or maintaining harbours; in which case the usage from time of memory was implied by the favour or the law without alleging it, when the service was alleged to be ancient or was from its nature ancient.   On the other hand when the right claimed was one against common right as common appurtenant, common by reason of vicinage or other right not specially favoured by the law, then they had to stand on the strength of their own titles, which had to be fully and accurately alleged.

An interesting case where the allegation was held unnecessary was *Lord Stanhope v. Ecquester*, Latch. 87, where a substantial part of the argument was directed to showing that it was one of those cases which, owing to the service rendered to the public, ought to be treated with favour by the law. It was an action upon the case brought by Lord Stanhope against Matthew de l'Equester concerning the fees of the postmaster. There were three objections to the declaration. The first of them was that it had stated that the office of postmaster was an ancient office, and that there were divers fees pertaining thereto for carrying letters as well from London to lands across the sea as from thence to London, but had not prescribed that these fees had been paid time out of mind. The plaintiff argued that that was not necessary, first, because he had declared that it was an ancient office, and secondly, because it was at the same time an office of that public benefit that it should be considered one of those cases where such allegation was implied. It was the duty of the office, and the office did actually carry, all letters passing to and from London and foreign parts, except such letters as were sent by friends or servants; and that service could not be performed for nothing. The fees charged were reasonable, being from London to Amsterdam, Antwerp and Hamburg 8*d.* per letter, and the same for letters thence to London. And it was held good.

Of course as pointed out before, where a thing follows by necessary implication from a fact alleged, so that there can really be no question whether it is averred or not, it need not be alleged. So it was held that a claim that a tenant for life adhuc seisita existit was sufficient without also alleging specially that she was still alive. *Scamber v. Johnson*, T. Jones, 227.

It is to be observed however that the Statute of Jeofails before referred to has a very important bearing upon technical objections of this kind. After issue taken and verdict found the want of all such allegations is aided by the Statute. It will be necessary to go into this subject a little in detail because it is rather complicated, and unless one has a clear understanding of it, it is impossible to see the ground of the decision in any case that may arise. Now it must be borne in mind that quite irrespective of any Statute of Jeofails, the Common Law of itself remedied certain defects of pleading after verdict found. "Where there is any defect, imperfection or omission in any pleading, whether in substance or form, which would have been a fatal objection: yet if the issue joined be such as necessarily required on the trial proof of the facts so defectively or imperfectly stated or omitted, and without which it is not to be presumed that either the judge would direct the jury to give, or the jury would have given the verdict, such defect, imperfection or omission is cured by the verdict by the Common Law." *Stennel v. Hogg*, 1 Saund. 227 n.

Thus when in debt for rent by a bargainee of a reversion, the declaration omitted to allege the attornment of the tenant which before the Statute 4 Anne, c. 16, section 9, was a necessary ceremony to complete the title of the bargainee, and upon nil debet pleaded there was a verdict for the plaintiff, such omission was cured by the verdict by the Common Law. *Hitchin v. Stevens*, 2 Show. p. 244.

So in an action for malicious prosecution it is necessary to allege in the declaration that the prosecution is at an end. *Waterer v. Freeman*, Hob. 267. But the want of this averment is cured after verdict, *Wine v. Ware*, 1 Sid. 15: though upon demurrer or after judgment by default the objection would be fatal, for the original prosecution might either be at an end or be still going on, and the Court would have no means of proving which is the fact. But where there is a verdict for the plaintiff, it is a necessary inference that it was proved at the trial that the prosecution was at an end, or there would certainly be reasonable and probable cause."

This was the extent of the aid of a verdict at Common Law, for where there was any defect, omission or imperfection, though in form only, in some collateral parts of the pleading that were not in issue between the parties, so that there was no room to presume that the defect or omission was supplied by proof, a verdict did not cure them at Common Law.

But as it was thought hard that after a cause had been

tried upon the merits, judgment should be stayed or reversed for defects in form in such collateral matters, the Statutes of Jeofails were passed: and their effect was by Statute 4 Anne, c. 16, section 2, extended to judgments by default. The meaning of the name is said to be that the pleader notices an error in his pleadings and acknowledges it (Jeo faile).

These Statutes are many in number and intricate in provisions. If I were writing a history of pleading it would be necessary to go into them in detail, but I must content myself here with enumerating them, and making one remark upon their effect. They begin in a long series from early times. They are :—Stat. 14 Edward III. c. 6: 9 Hen. V. c. 4: 4 Hen. VI. c. 3: 8 Hen. VI. c. 12 and 15: 32 Hen. VIII. c. 30: 18 Eliz. c. 14: 21 Jac. I. c. 13: 16 and 17 Car. II. c. 8: 4 and 5 Anne, c. 16: 9 Anne, c. 20: 5 Geo. I. c. 13. These all provide for various points other than those helped by a verdict at Common Law. The one remark upon them that I wish to make is this, arising out of the construction of the Statute 4 Anne, c. 16, section 2. That section provides as follows: "All the Statutes of Jeofails shall be extended to judgments by default in any court of record, and no such judgment shall be reversed for or by reason of any imperfection, omission, defect, matter or thing whatsoever, *which would have been aided or cured by any of the said Statutes of Jeofails* in case a verdict of twelve men had been given in the said action or suit." Now upon the construction of this section it was decided, see *Vandeput v. Lord*, 1 Str. 78, *Hayes v. Warren*, 2 Str. 933, *Collins v. Gibbs*, 2 Burr. 899, that it extends to protect judgments by default against such objections only as are remedied after a verdict *by the Statutes of Jeofails*, and not against objections cured by a verdict at Common Law. Hence wherever the question arose with reference to a judgment by default it was necessary to determine whether the defect was one remediable by verdict at Common Law or by the Statutes.

This necessity seems to have escaped the attention of Blackstone, for after stating the principle upon which verdicts are at Common Law an aid to defects (3 Comm. 394—), he adduces two examples, both of which are instances of defects aided by Statutes of Jeofails.

And it is curious that the reporter of a judgment of Lord Hardwicke in *R. v. Bishop of Llandaff*, 2 St. 1006, is under the same misconception. That was a quare impedit. The declaration alleged a seisin in the Crown of the advowson, but no presentation. The seisin was traversed and a verdict found for the Crown. Upon the question whether the want of allegation of presentation was cured by the verdict, Lord Hardwicke is reported as saying that it was so cured by virtue of 16 and 17 Car. II., c. 8. But it is obvious that the ground of the decision was that it was cured by the verdict at Common Law, since a presentation must of necessity have been proved upon the trial, otherwise the jury could not have found a seisin in the Crown.

So in the principal case *Stennel v. Hogg*, Saund. 225 a, it was held that where a prescriptive right of common is pleaded and put in issue, and there is a verdict in favour of the right, the want of averring that the plaintiff's cattle were in that part of the land in which the common is claimed, or that the cattle were levant and couchant upon the plaintiff's land, is aided by the Statutes of Jeofails.

See too *Hall v. Marshall*, Cro. Car. 497 : Vin. *Ab.* Pres. 288, citing G. *Hist. of C. B.* 113.

In claiming common, care is necessary to claim exactly the right that one has, or, if one has various rights arising in different ways, one ought to make separate claims for each, and not lump the whole together.

Thus in *Basket v. Lord Mordaunt*, Dyer, 164, it was held that if a man has common in a down or waste for 100 sheep as appurtenant to a messuage and certain acres of land meadow and pasture, and he purchases another messuage with certain land which has also common appurtenant in the same waste for another 100 sheep by prescription, he must not, in pleading, claim a common appurtenant to both messuages and lands together for 200 sheep : but he must make two separate prescriptive titles each for 100 sheep, for they are two distinct commons.

So it would seem (*Gregory v. Hill*, Cro. Eliz. 531) that if a man claims simply common appurtenant to his house and 20 acres of land: when ten of them are freehold and ten copyhold, that is not a good allegation. And it was then said that the same would hold supposing that part of the land had been copyhold 100 years before but had been enfranchised and was then his freehold.

But on the other hand, *Potter v. North*, Lev. 268, where a man pleads that there are divers freehold and copyhold tenements within the manor, and that he is seised of a freehold tenement there, and that he and other freeholders, and all those whose estates they have, time out of mind &c., together with the copyholders, have had solam et separalem pasturam: and then pleads a custom that the copyholders together with the freeholders, time whereof &c. have had the same right, that was held good pleading on the authority of a case between *Kettleborough v. Wells*, Trin. 1654, Rot. 549.

So in a case of *Conyers v. Jackson*, in Clayton's *Reports of York Assizes*, p. 19, pl. 32, it is laid down that when a man hath an acre of freehold in a great field to which common doth belong he cannot in his prescription lay it that he hath common in the whole field, but in such a part of the field, as in that toward the east part or the west part of the field. Because if otherwise he would be extending his prescription to his own land, which would not be good.

But in *Hickman v. Thorny*, Freem. 210, *Sir Miles Corbet's Case*, 7 Co. fol. 5, p. 57, is cited as showing that it is a good prescription when a man has lands lying intermixed in a common field to say that he has common in all the fields except his own lands.

There are two cases which certainly illustrate the niceties of pleading in earlier times, in one of which the defect was held to be a mere matter of form and so not fatal, while in the other the defect was a fatal one of substance.

In *Harvey and Corydon v. Willoughby*, Freem. 19, the plaintiffs entitled themselves, to each of them a mill, and declared that they had used to repair the said mills; and prescribed that all the inhabitants within the manor had used to grind omne frumentum that they spent at their mills or at the mills of one of them. This was held bad for two reasons. It should have been alleged that all the corn not ground at the mill of A used to be ground at the mill of B, and that all the corn not ground at the mill of B used to be ground at the mill of A. For, as it was alleged, one of the two plaintiffs might have no right, since the allegation that all the inhabitants were bound to grind at the mills of A and B or one of them, was quite consistent with none of them ever grinding at the mill of B. But one cannot help thinking that the same objection applies to the count as amended by Hale, C. J. The second objection is perhaps more valid. It was that the prescription to grind omne frumentum spent in the house was bad as too wide, for it might well be that they spent corn which was never ground at all, as e.g. what was given to the pigs and hens or made into frumenty. The prescription therefore should have been to grind omnia grana molienda. To the same effect is *Upjohn v. Conduit*, Freem. 459, and see *John Harbin and Uxor v. Green*, Hob. 189, when such a custom was held unreasonable on the ground that it could apply to all corn bought away from the land, and not only corn growing on the land.

The other case in which the plea was held good certainly seems in accordance with common sense.

In *Mellor v. Walker*, 2 Saund. 4, the defendant in trespass justified at another time than the time in the declaration, but alleged it to be the same trespass of which the plaintiff complained. And this was held good in substance, being if anything only a matter of form. (See the notes to that case in Saunders where the subject is considered at length.) Of course where a prescription is alleged in rent or common, and the plea is unity of possession of the rent or common and the land out of which it issues, this is a sufficient plea without traversing the continuance of the prescription. Brook, *Ab.* Traverse, pl. 185, Y. B. 5 H. VII. 11.

CHAPTER X.

What Finding will support a Prescription.

Assuming that no objection of form can be taken to the claim, within what limits may the facts proved exceed or fall short of the right so claimed without prejudice to the right to judgment upon the claim?

Now the case with regard to a finding of more or less of the same kind as the right claimed seems rather peculiar. It was held in *Gregory v. Hill*, Cro. Eliz. 531, that if a man prescribed to have common appurtenant to his house and 20 acres of land, and it is found that he has a house and 18 acres only; still he has substantiated his claim, and it will stand for the 18 acres.

But in *Bushwood v. Bond*, Cro. Eliz. 722, it was said by Walmsley that if a man prescribes for common for 100 sheep, and the jury finds he has common for 120 sheep, *i.e.* more of the same kind, he has not made out his claim. But it was held in the same case that where he had claimed common for 100 sheep and the jury had found for him common for 100 sheep and 6 cows, i.e. more but of a different kind, his prescription was good. So too in *Davies v. Stephens*, 7 C. and P. 570, where plaintiff claimed a footway and the jury found a carriageway, that was held to support the claim. And in *Gregory v. Hill, ubi sup.* it was also held that the claim being for common for 20 acres, if it had been found that the 20 acres were composed partly of freehold and partly of copyhold, *i.e.* though of the same total amount, yet of different kinds, that would have been bad. Though that may have been rather upon the other ground, that there was no allegation of the custom for the copyhold. But the case of *Mitchell v. Mortimer*, Hob. 209, seems rather hard to distinguish from *Gregory v. Hill*. At any rate, it shows that a finding of less than has been claimed will

only support the prescription when there are no other circumstances of difference, and the question is simply one of more
or less.

In *Mitchell v. Mortimer*, Mitchell brought a replevin against
Mortimer, and issue was taken whether John Mitchell and all
those whose estate etc. had used to have common for all their
beasts levant and couchant upon a messuage, 200 acres of land,
50 of meadow and 50 of pasture in four towns.   The jury
found that Mitchell was seised of the house, land, meadow and
pasture in the same four towns, but that he had his common
as belonging only to the messuage and 200 acres of land, 20
of meadow and 20 of pasture in two only of the towns.   Judgment was given upon this finding against the plaintiff on the
ground that it did not support his claim.

As to a finding of more than is claimed the judgment in
Johnson v. Thoroughgood, Brownlow and Gold. 177, is useful.   It is
there said that if a man have common for great cattle and sheep,
and the sheep be taken damage feasant, and he prescribes that
he has common for sheep only, and the jury find common for sheep
and great cattle, the common is found for the plaintiff.   And
the like if one claim common all the time of the year, when
the land lies fallow, and when it is sown, from such a day unto
etc.; and his cattle are taken in the year when it is sown or
lies fallow, it is sufficient for the plaintiff to prescribe for
common either in the year when it is sown, or when it lies
fallow, according to which it was at the time the cattle were
taken.   Then if the jury find all the common it is sufficiently
found for the plaintiff.

And the reason of this is given in the judgment of the
Court in *Bruges v. Searle and another*, Carthew 219.   In trespass for impounding sheep, the prescription was for common
for all his sheep.   Issue was taken upon the prescription, and
there was a special verdict to this effect, "that the Plaintiff
had common of pasture there for all his sheep prout interius
placidando allegavit, sed iidem juratores ulterius dicunt that
the Plaintiff hath common there as well for all other cattle
levant and couchant on his tenement as for sheep, as appurtenant to his said tenement."

The Court held that this was a general verdict for the plaintiff, because the jury had found that the plaintiff had common prout allegavit, and all the matter found afterwards was surplusage and void. But the Court went on to give their general opinion that the reason the verdict was found for the plaintiff was this, that the action was only for impounding sheep, and therefore the plaintiff might well abridge his prescription, so as to claim common for them only, since nothing else was in dispute; and the finding that he had common for other cattle did not falsify his prescription but stood well with it. It will be readily seen now that the rules as to what finding of more or less than what is claimed supports a prescription, rest upon a logical basis. A man cannot succeed in a prescription where it is more than he has claimed. At first sight one cannot quite understand why the finding should not support the prescription to the extent of the claim; so that if a man prescribed for common for 100 sheep and the jury found for 120, that should be good for 100. But the reason would appear to be that this was not the way provided by the law for stinting commons. And there would have always been the danger that even after that the man would have continued to use his common for the amount of the finding rather than the amount of the claim. Certainly the plaintiff was put to no disadvantage, because it was his own fault if he did not succeed as to the full amount of his right, by claiming, in case of doubt, more than he was entitled to, and in that case getting the benefit of the converse rule that the claim would be established to the amount of the finding, where that was less than the claim.

But it must be observed that a claimant will only get the benefit of this rule apparently, where his claim has exceeded his right in numbers, and not where it has exceeded in point of time, or even where the question is in substance one of number only, if the claim has been excessive as regards the right in respect of which they were claimed. As regards a claim excessive in point of time this was held in *Rex v. Inhabitants of Hermitage*, Carth. 241. There the prescription had been for common of pasture in Hermitage Common for all cattle levant and couchant upon their tenements at all times of the year. The finding was for the prescription, with the difference only that sheep were excepted for some part of the year. Upon this the Court resolved that the finding would not support the plea; and that the prescription ought to have been pleaded specially with this exception. The second point is established by the case of the *Count of Devon v. Eyre*, Palm. 362, when it was held that a prescription for sheep levant and couchant was not maintained by a finding for sheep levant and couchant, but only those belonging to the plaintiff. I think the exact words of the report in Palmer give the judgment most quaintly and succinctly: "Le 2 matter fuit quia le prescription est pro ovibus and le proof fall out d'estre, que ont, pur ses proper barbits tantum, and pur lack de parol (suis) fuit object, que le evidence ne maintaine le prescription. Et de ceo opinion fuit tout le Court: Quia per prescription barbits in agistment, ou auterment levant and couchant doent aver common que n'est warranted per le proofe; quia dit que ad common pur ses proper barbits tantum; et pur ceo reason le defendant fuit trouve culp."

Nor apparently does the rule apply where the claim has been excessive by reason that a part of the original right has been released. Thus in *Rotheram v. Green*, Noy. 67, in an action of trespass against Green he justifies because of a common appendant by prescription in 500 acres. It was found by the verdict that his ancestor had released his common in five of these acres. The Court held that the prescription had failed. But this was apparently only for purposes of the action of trespass. For the Court went on to say that the common by that is not extinct because it is discharged to be common by Act of Parliament for fayler of prescription.

A distinction well worth noting is that taken in *Gray's Case*, 5 Rep. 78 a.

There in replevin between Gray and Fletcher in bar of the Avowry for damage feasance, the plaintiff by custom intitled himself to have common of pasture in the place where etc. to his copyhold. It was found that he ought to have the same common, but that every copyholder had used to pay time out of mind, etc. one hen and five eggs annually. It was held that on this finding the plaintiff should have judgment, for he is not bound to allege more than makes for him, and is of his part. The meaning of that is this, that the jury had found two distinct prescriptions, one for the common, and a counter prescription of the lord for the hen and eggs. If the finding had been for the common, but only upon terms of paying the hen and the eggs, the judgment would have been against the plaintiff, because he would then have failed to allege a necessary part of his claim. This appears clear from the case of the pot water cited by Popham Chief Justice as a Devonshire case. A man had prescribed to have pot water out of the river, and the jury had found that he ought to have it, paying sixpence yearly. Whereupon it was adjudged that he had failed in his prescription, for he had prescribed absolutely, and the jury had found it conditionally. The same result was arrived at in *Lovelace v. Reynolds,* Noy. 59, where a defendant prescribed for common, and it was found that he ought to have it, paying 1*d.* yearly to the plaintiff. And also in *Brigandine v. Westan* at the assise in Kent, cited *ib.*; where one prescribed to have a way to a church, and it was found that he ought to have a way paying every year to the terre tenant 2*d.* and a pair of gloves for everyone that he should marry out of his house.

It should be noted, however, in these cases, that the question whether the finding is a finding of two prescriptions or a finding of one conditional prescription does not depend upon the mere accident of the language in which the jury have expressed themselves, but is a matter of substance. The real point to be noted is whether the person having the right to the counter prescription has any separate remedy for it, or whether his only remedy is to disturb the enjoyment of the first prescriptive right. In *Gray's Case, sup.* what was said upon that point was this:—"The doubt was what remedy the terre tenant should have for the hens and eggs; for if the terre tenant has no remedy for them, then the commoner should have his common sub modo scil. paying so much etc. and then it would be against the plaintiff. But if the terre tenant has a good remedy for the hens and eggs, then as the verdict is found it is not a modus communiae nor parcel of the issue as to the common, but a collateral recompense to be paid for the common whereof everyone has equal remedy."

There are several cases which show in a most striking way the application of the rule that when a right has been prescribed for the user found in fact or admitted must not exceed the right so claimed. In *Webster v. Bach*, Freem. 246, C. 259, in trespass the defendant justified by a prescription for a way to a certain close. It does not appear whether the way was merely a foot-way, or whether it included a carriage and cart-way. I think it may be assumed that the latter was the case, since it would be so obvious an excess of the prescription to use a foot-way as a carriage-way. The plaintiff replied that the defendant had brought along the way a load of hay which had grown upon another close than that in respect of which the prescription was laid. The defendant demurred, which was of course tantamount to an admission of the fact. It was adjudged against him, for a private way to a close cannot be enlarged to other purposes.

So a private carriage-way from A to B cannot be used for the purpose of going from A to C, although B adjoins C and lies in the way to it, 1 Rol. 391. And an analogous case is *Howell v. King*, Mod. 190, a case of trespass for driving cattle over the plaintiff's ground. It appeared that A had a way over B's ground to Blackacre. He drove his beasts along the way over B's ground to Blackacre, and thence drove them on to another adjoining field beyond. It was argued upon demurrer that the beasts were lawfully driven to Blackacre, and that when they were there, they might lawfully be driven anywhere else. But the Court agreed with the argument of the plaintiff that if that were so, it would also hold supposing A purchased 1000 acres adjoining Blackacre: that the right to the way to Blackacre was a prescriptive right, and therefore supposed a grant, and that as no grant of the way to the newly-acquired 1000 acres could be supposed, the prescription could not be extended to allow a way to them.

Exactly the same principle is followed in the decision of *Laughton v. Ward*, Lutw. 111.

There a man prescribed for a way through Badsley Well

Lane to Badsley Well Close, and it was admitted that he had used that way, but had gone on from the close to another close called Waiter Langdalls. The Court held that the prescription did not justify the additional user.

But the converse proposition is illustrated by *Bruerton v. Right*, Freem. p. 51, c. 63, which shows that the owner of a servient tenement cannot restrict a prescription of user from a certain event till a certain event, by bringing about any other than the exact event of the prescription. In trespass in that case the defendant justified for common from the carrying away of the corn until the land was re-sowed with grain. It was held that a planting with turnips would not do.

See too *Murgatroid v. Law*, Carth. 117.

The cases where the finding is not exactly the same as the right claimed, but yet is held to be in substance a finding for the claim, are numerous, and illustrate the triumph of common sense over strict technicality. To take one or two examples. There are several given in Jenkin's Reports, first century, case 21.

Thus where a tenant prescribed for an acquittal against his lord, and it was found that the lord and his ancestors had acquitted the tenant and his ancestors from time of memory, but had omitted to do so in the time of the tenant and his grandfather, that finding was held to support the prescription.

So *ib.*, where upon a prescription for a modus decimandi way or common the verdict finds no modus way or common for twenty or forty years, but that before that, from time of memory, there was such modus way or common, that maintains the prescription. So when a lease is pleaded as having been granted for 30 years from 30th March, 1 James, and the verdict finds it was granted 28th March, 1 James, for 30 years, the substance of the plea is found.

And again where an account settled before two auditors is pleaded, it is found to have been before only one, that is good, as the number of auditors is not of substance for the allowance or disallowance of an account.

So in *Sir Thomas Danby's Case*, Clayt. 54, in trespass a

prescription was to tether equos and boves upon such a balke which was the place where the trespass was laid. If he use this with mares or cows that will be justified by the prescription. For the ox and horse are but instances, and he is not tied up to exactly that kind of beasts in his plea. For the main substance of the matter is that the grass has been eaten by him.

But an earlier case, *Stapleton v. Morse*, Cro. Eliz. 798, is apparently inconsistent with this. There in replevin for taking one horse, one gelding, and two cows, the prescription was for common for all horses, cows and pigs, and the defendant demurred as the prescription did not cover geldings. And of that opinion was Anderson, who held that stone horses and geldings are several, and therefore ought to be prescribed for separately. And the rest of the Court were evidently of opinion that the thing was different in substance, for although they held that the prescription for horses covered geldings, that was on the ground that the word horse in itself in fact meant gelding, and not on the broad ground that the claim was in substance the same. This appears clear from the fact that they held that the prescription for horses did not cover mares : certainly, one would have thought the same in substance ; and certainly inconsistent with Sir Thomas Danby's Case.

With regard to ways it should be noted that a public way is not gained by prescription but by dedication, which may be express or implied ; and generally is implied from a user by all persons indiscriminately for a comparatively short time. Thus three or four years have, in special circumstances, been held a sufficient time ; see *Trustees of Rugby Charity v. Merryweather*, 11 East, 375 : *Jarvis v. Dean*, 3 Bing. 447, *R. v. Hudson*, Str. 909.

But it must not be forgotten that the owner of the land still retains the right to use the land for all purposes not inconsistent with the right of passage of the public. So that the appropriation of one part as a paved footpath does not prevent him from committing what would be a nuisance by bringing heavy machinery over it on to his land. *Vestry of St Mary Newington v. Jacobs*, L. R. 7 Q. B. 47.

The question whether a public and private right of way can co-exist over the same soil is important for this reason, that the remedy for obstruction of a public way is by indictment, and no action will lie unless the plaintiff has suffered some peculiar damage above the rest of the public. The law seems to be that if a public way exists no private right of way can be acquired, *R. v. Chorley*, 12 Q. B. 515, but where the private right exists it is not necessarily merged in a subsequently acquired public one, *Allen v. Ormond*, 8 East 3, *Duncan v. Louch*, 6 Q. B. 915, though it may be, *Chichester v. Lethbridge*, Willes 71.

Where there is a public highway the owners of land adjoining have a right of access to it at all parts. This is a private right for obstruction of which an action will lie. *Lyon v. Fishmongers' Company*, 1 App. Cas. 662: *Fritz v. Hobson*, 14 Ch. D. 542.

CHAPTER XI.

How Prescriptive Rights are Destroyed or Lost.

PRESCRIPTIVE rights can of course be put an end to in various ways. Thus they can be extinguished by Act of Parliament either directly, or, as is most often the case, incidentally in the course of the construction of works under the powers of some Act of Parliament. In these Acts the Lands Clauses Consolidation Act are almost invariably embodied, and the question of compensation to the owners of rights thereby injured is decided under the provisions of that Act. But it is to be noticed that an Act authorising works to be constructed is only to be construed as extinguishing prescriptive rights that it specially includes. Thus in an important case, *Clark v. London School Board*, 9 Ch. 120, when the London School Board under the compulsory powers of the Elementary Education Act 1870 had acquired the freehold in a piece of land and was proceeding to build a school upon it so as to block up the ancient lights of the plaintiff, an owner of adjoining houses whose interest had not been acquired by the defendants, it was held that his remedy was not merely for compensation under the Lands Clauses Act, but that he was entitled to an injunction restraining the Board from continuing the building until it had acquired the plaintiff's interest in the houses.

Of course the cases as to compensation under the Act are too numerous to be dealt with here, but it may be well just to notice two very recent cases in which the doctrine has been extended to prescriptive rights merely inchoate. The first of these is *Re an arbitration between the London, Tilbury and Southend Railway Company and the Trustees of the Gower's Walk Schools*, 24 Q. B. D. 40, 326. There the claimant being the owner of certain buildings with ancient lights pulled them down and erected a new building on their site. The position of certain portions of the windows of the new building coincided with that of portions of the old windows, while other portions of the new windows occupied wholly different positions. Before any right to the access of light to the non-coinciding portions of the new windows had been acquired, a railway company in the exercise of their powers erected a warehouse which obstructed the lights of windows in the new building.

Held that the claimant was entitled to compensation in respect of the whole of the windows so obstructed, including the *windows and portions of windows which did not coincide with any of the ancient lights.*

The other case to which I wish to refer upon this point is *Barlow v. Ross*, 24 Q. B. D. 381.

That is a case arising under the Artizans and Labourers' Dwellings Improvement Act, 1875. The 20th section of that Act provides that upon the purchase by the local authority of any lands required for the purpose of carrying into effect an improvement scheme under the Act, "All rights of way, rights of laying down or of continuing any pipes, sewers or drains, on through, or under such lands, and all rights or easements in or relating to such lands shall be extinguished," subject to payment of compensation. It was held that that section included cases where a right or easement is in process of being acquired by enjoyment under the Prescription Act at the date of the purchase of the land, and that it had the effect of extinguishing such inchoate rights as well as rights or easements already acquired over such land. It was held therefore that the owner of a house to which there had been access of lights over land purchased by a local authority under the Act for the period of ten years before and ten years after such purchase did not gain an easement of light under the Prescription Act by reason of such twenty years' enjoyment, and semble he would be entitled to compensation to the extent to which the value of his house might be diminished by the operation of the section.

So prescriptive rights might be put an end to by operation of law, or by the act of the owner: which may be by release, actual or presumed, or by abandonment. But when a right has been once acquired it is indefeasible by any act of parties other than the owner of the right, see *Selby v. Nettlefold*, 9 Ch. 111, and *Horne v. Taylor*, Noy, 128.

The most frequent case of the extinction of prescriptive rights by operation of law is by unity of seisin. But the first point which it is necessary to very carefully notice in this connexion is whether the right in question is a right acquired by prescription, or whether it is a natural right belonging to a person by the mere ownership of his land and which can only be interfered with by a person who had gained a prescriptive right to disturb it. The best illustration of this is the right with regard to which the question actually arose for decision, viz. a natural stream. That was in the well-known case of *Sury v. Pigot*, Popham 166, Tudor's *Lead. Cas.* 'Conv.'

There A was possessed of a rectory of which a curtilage was parcel. From time immemorial a watering-place for cattle existed in the said curtilage, and a stream had flowed through a piece of land called the hopyard to fill the pond at the watering-place. A afterwards purchased the hopyard, and thus became possessed of the rectory and hopyard at the same time. He then sold the hopyard to B, under whose title the defendant entered, and obstructed the water-course. It was held that the right to the water-course was not extinguished by the unity of possession. Doddridge, J. there says,

"For the matter of law, I conceive that the unity of possession doth not extinguish the water-course for two reasons :—

"(1) For the necessity of the thing...as there is a necessity of bread, so in our case there is a necessity of water. And for the case of a way distinguendum est. For if it be a way which is only for easement, it is extinguished by unity of possession : but if it be a way of necessity, as a way to market or church, there it is not extinguished by unity of possession (see *Large v. Pitt*, Peake, *Ad. Ca.* 153).

"(2) From the nature of water, which naturally descends. It is always current and aut invenit aut facit viam ; and shall such a thing be extinguished which hath its being from the creation ?"

Where however the right was one gained by grant or pre-

H.   13

scription it is merged and extinguished by unity of possession. Co. Litt. 114 b.

There is a class of cases, viz. that of easements of necessity, or continuous or apparent easements, which is often treated as an exception to this rule, and spoken of as if they were only suspended during the unity of possession and revived on the severance. But it is better to treat them as new created: a grant being implied of everything without which the thing granted could not be used. See *Pheysey v. Vicary*, 16 M. and W. 491, *Holmes v. Goring*, 2 Bing. 76. And they arise not only as against the grantor but also in his favour, see *Pinnington v. Galland*, 9 Ex. 1, *Davis v. Sear*, 7 Eq. 427.

See too among the numerous cases *Palmer v. Fleshies*, 1 Siderf. 167 : *Brown v. Alabaster*, 37 Ch. D. 490: *Kelk v. Pearson*, 6 Ch. 813.

Easements of necessity only arise where there is a grant, not where severance takes place otherwise, *e.g.* under Statute of Limitations. *Wilkes v. Greenway*, *Times*, July 30, 1890. But the grantor cannot derogate from his own grant, so that even when he has ancient lights in a building on the land retained by him he cannot prevent the purchaser from blocking up those ancient lights, *Ellis v. Manchester Carriage Coy.*, 2 C. P. D. 13; *White v. Bass*, 7 H. and N. 722. And unless the two plots of land are sold at the same auction the purchaser of the piece first sold can block up the windows of the later purchaser from the vendor. *Wheeldon v. Burrows*, 12 Ch. D. 31. Unless from the circumstances a reservation of the right is to be implied; *Russell v. Watts*, 10 App. Cas. 590. But the maxim that a grantor cannot derogate does not entitle a grantor of a house to claim an easement of light to an extent inconsistent with the intention to be implied from the circumstances existing at the time of the grant and known to the grantee, *Birmingham Bank v. Ross*, 38 Ch. D. 295; see too *Myers v. Catterson*, 43 Ch. D. 470. The implication of the grant is not prevented by the fact that the dominant tenement is in lease at the time of the alienation, and so not in the possession of the alienor, *Barnes v. Loach*, 4 Q. B. D. 494. And it is apparently the contract and not the mere conveyance that determines the question of right. Thus if the owner of a house and land contracts to sell the land, *then sells the house, then completes the sale of the land, the purchaser of the land gains the priority: and the purchaser of the house is held to have no right of light over the land. Beddington v. Attlee,* 35 Ch. D. 317.

It is to be observed with regard to extinction by unity, that it is not every unity of possession that will suffice, it must be unity of seisin. Unity of ownership of a dominant and servient tenement for different estates merely causes suspension and not extinction. And the seisin must be " of as high and perdurable estate."

Thus in *James v. Plant,* 4 A. and E. at p. 761, the Court said "we all agree that where there is unity of seisin of the land and of the way over the land in one and the same person, the right of way is either extinguished or suspended according to the duration of the respective estates in the land and the way."

And it would appear that the seisin must be a seisin in fee. The right is acquired as an adjunct to a dominant tenement. Now while the servient tenement is in the possession of the dominant owner the right is enjoyed not as an adjunct to the dominant tenement, but as one of the incidents of the possession of the servient tenement. If therefore the seisin be not a seisin in fee, the right which was attached to the dominant tenement over the servient tenement in remainder, or to the remainder of the dominant tenement over the servient tenement comes into operation. In *James v. Plant, sup.* the dominant tenement was vested in two sisters as coparceners in fee claiming by descent from their father. The servient estate came to them in tail general under the marriage settlement of the mother. It was held that a right of way was suspended during the unity of seisin; and that the suspension would continue until the unity of seisin ceased by the determination of the estate tail.

Unity of seisin is the important point, even where there is no unity of possession. Extinction will be effected where there is unity of seisin even where there is no unity of possession, as *e.g.* where one tenement is in possession of a tenant. *Buckley v. Coles,* 5 Taunt. 315.

Again, with regard to easements of necessity. It is now

13—2

well established that an easement of necessity is destroyed by operation of law so soon as the necessity which was the cause of its creation comes to an end. This may at first sight seem somewhat inconsistent with the principle that an easement when once acquired is indefeasible. That principle of course holds good of rights granted or gained by user simpliciter and not sub modo. But an easement of necessity is founded upon an implied grant with reference to the necessity, *i.e.* to continue so long as the necessity requires.

Holmes v. Elliott, 2 Bing. 76, is the case where that was decided. A note of Sergeant Williams was quoted in the judgment of Best, C. J., where he says:—

"A way of necessity, when the nature of it is considered, will be found to be nothing else than a way by grant," and says Best, C. J. "it is a grant of no more than the circumstances which raise the implication of necessity require should pass." And again in reply to a somewhat fallacious argument that had been used, viz. that the effect of the new implied grant was to prevent the extinguishment of the old right of way, Sergeant Williams is quoted, "Where a man having a close surrounded with his own land grants the close to another, the grantee shall have a way to the close over the grantor's land, as incident to the grant, for without it he cannot derive any benefit from the grant. So it is when he grants the land and reserves the close to himself." And upon that Best, C. J., commenting says, "What way is it the grantee shall have? Not the old, but a new way, limited by the necessity." Of course the general principle that where a right is granted for a particular time, or for a particular purpose, and the time is ended, or the purpose accomplished, the grant is exhausted and comes to an end, is a principle so agreeable to common sense, and so well-established in our law, as to require no authority. But it does not always appear at first sight whether a case comes within the rule or no. An instructive case of this kind is *National Guaranteed Manure Company v. Donald*, 4 H. and N. 8. That was a case where a Company had been incorporated by Act of Parliament for the purpose of making a canal. The Act provided that the Company should have power to supply the canal with water from certain rivers by means of a cut, which thus constituted an easement over the lands of other persons. Some time after the Canal Company was reconstituted by another Act as a Railway Company, and thereupon demised to the plaintiffs the property and rights they possessed in respect of the canal. The question was whether the plaintiffs had acquired by the demise the right to the easement of conducting water over the defendant's land by means of the cut. Now it had been established by the case of *Rochdale Canal Company v. Radcliffe*, 18 Q. B. 287, that a parliamentary corporation is a corporation for the purposes only for which it has been established by Parliament, and has no existence for any other purpose: it was therefore held that when the Canal Company ceased to be a Company for using a canal the easement which had been created only for the purpose of use with the canal came to an end: and that therefore the Company had had nothing they could convey to the plaintiffs, and that the plaintiffs had no right.

There is a class of cases depending upon the same principle as this, where very fine distinctions are taken despite the fact that the broad ground of decision applicable to them all is well established and easily laid down. These are cases where a right having been acquired for user in respect of a certain dominant tenement such right has, by the alteration of the dominant tenement, become incapable of user in precisely the same way as before. In such cases the question arises whether the right can be used at all, and whether it is some entirely new right that is claimed. And this must evidently depend upon the extent of the alteration of the dominant tenement. Now it is quite clear that a mere trifling alteration will not affect the right. On the other hand when the alteration has been such as to entirely alter the character of the right claimed it is equally clear that the right is destroyed. The difficulty lies in the application.

The general rule is nowhere better laid down than by Grove, J., in *Harvey v. Walters*, L. R., 8 C. P. at p. 166. "It appears to us that to hold that any, even the slightest, variation in the enjoyment of an easement would destroy the easement, would virtually do away with all easements, as by the effect of natural causes some change must take place. Thus water percolating or flowing would produce some wear-and-tear, and alter the height or width of the conduit; so would weather, alterations of heat and cold, &c. In the case of ancient lights changes in the transparency of glass, wear-and-tear of frames, growth of shrubs, &c. would produce effects which would vary the character of the enjoyment. In the user of a footpath the footsteps would never be on the same line or confined accurately to the same width of road. We are of opinion that the question here, as in *Hall v. Swift* and other cases, is whether there has been a substantial variance in the mode of, or extent of user, or enjoyment of the easement, so as to throw a greater burden on the servient tenement. In the language of Sir R. Kindersley, which was adopted by the M. R. in *Heath v. Bucknell,* there must be an additional or different servitude, and the change must be material either *in the nature or in the quantum of the servitude imposed."* This is the real test: and it is obviously consistent with the nature of prescriptive rights, depending as they do on a presumed grant. It is clear that a grant of a right in respect of a tenement will not extend to a case where such an alteration of the dominant tenement has taken place that the tenement or the mode of user of the right is substantially changed in character. As was said by Willes, J., in *Williams v. James,* L. R., 2 C. P. at p. 582, " the user must be the reasonable use for the purposes of the land in the condition in which it was while the user took place." In that case he also said with respect to a right of way to a field, " I quite agree also with the argument that the right of way can only be used for the field in its ordinary use as a field. The right could not be used for a manufactory built upon the field."

An important case is *Allan v. Gomme,* 11 A. and E. 758, where it was held that a right of way to a shed used as a wood-house was not lost by the wood-house being converted to some other purpose; the description being merely for the purpose of ascertaining the locality: but that the way could only be used so long as the place remained substantially in the same condition. What amount and kind of alteration is permissible is indicated from the opinion of Parke, B., in *Henning v. Burnet*, 8 Ex. 187, where he thought that if a right of way were granted to be used as a way to a cottage the right would cease if the cottage were changed to a tanyard: but that it would not be lost by alterations in the cottage. But at the best a question depending upon the view of the Court as to the amount of change must be one of very great uncertainty. This will very well appear from *R. v. Tippett*, 3 B. and Ald. 193, where one would think the decision might well be either way. That was a question as to the right of way of the public over a towing-path at the side of a river. The river had been tidal, and consequently the path was only used at high tide. The river was afterwards altered so as to become navigable at all times: and it was thereupon contended that as the right would then be so greatly increased in amount it was really not the same right as had been gained and that the old right was lost. But the Court was of a contrary opinion, and held that the right extended to a user at all times, on the ground that the right was from the beginning a right of user at all times, and had been limited, not by the ordinance of man, but by natural causes; that it was an absolute right which had in fact been only used at certain times because it was impracticable at others.

Of course it is clear that if a right gained either by user, or as would be more frequently the case, by express grant, is a right to use for all purposes and under all conditions, no alteration of the dominant tenement can make any difference to it.

Another way in which prescriptive rights are lost is by the act of the owner.

Now of course such rights may be extinguished by express release by the owner. Such release must be by deed since the right can only be expressly created by deed.

But of course there may be an implied release. And it is to be observed that it is under this head of implied release that all the cases of so-called abandonment should be classed. Thus in *Lovell v. Smith*, 3 C. B. N. S. p. 127, Willes, J., says:—" I do not think that this Court means to lay it down that there can be an abandonment of a prescriptive easement like this without a deed or evidence from which the jury can presume a release of it."

Now with regard to this implied release the question is, has the conduct of the owner been such as to show an intention not to use the right again, or rather, since there is often nothing to guide one as to the intention, has the conduct of the owner been such as to induce other people to believe, and to act on the belief, that he never intended to use the right again? If it was then he will be brought within the doctrine of estoppel.

Now any evidence of an intention to abandon is sufficient; but in practice it most frequently happens that there really is no evidence of intention at all save the mere fact that the right has not been exercised: and that probably because it was not required. Now it is clear that mere non-user for a great length of time is not sufficient to destroy a prescriptive right; see *Seaman v. Vawdry*, 16 Ves. 390, where there had been non-user for 106 years. On the other hand non-user of such a nature as is found to imply an intention of abandonment is not required to continue for any definite length of time. It proceeds upon the theory of a release and the destruction is completed at once. See *R. v. Chorley*, 12 Q. B. at p. 518.

And of course supposing the right in question has never been the subject of an action, so far as the Prescription Act is concerned, as has been previously pointed out, non-user for one year prior to the action will defeat the right, not on the ground of abandonment, but upon the ground that under the Act the right has never been gained. But here *Hollins v. Verney*, 13 Q. B. D. 314, must be borne in mind.

It frequently happens that the reason for the non-user of a prescriptive right is some agreement between a dominant and a servient owner that the right shall not be exercised. It is clear then that the presumption of abandonment is rebutted by such agreement. The only point requiring notice in the circumstances is that when the non-user by the dominant owner is the correlative of an user by the servient owner of a contrary right, in all cases coming under the Prescription Act such contrary right will not be prevented from being acquired and becoming indefeasible by the agreement unless the agreement be by deed or in writing.

It has also been held (see *Hale v. Oldroyd*, 14 M. and W.

789) that where the non-user of a right is due to the fact that the substantial benefit of the right was, during the period of non-user, enjoyed through the substitution for convenience of another mode of enjoyment, in such a case the non-user raises no presumption of abandonment.

It must be borne in mind too that the exercise of a prescriptive right is an exercise for the benefit of the owner alone ; and that such exercise is no representation to anybody else that the user will be continued, so as to make the owner liable in equity to compensate anybody for damage suffered through acting upon the representation.   The user may be discontinued at any time regardless of the effect upon the rights of other people.   An excellent instance of this is afforded by *Mason v. Shrewsbury and Hereford Ry. Co.*, L. R. 3 Q. B. 579.   There a Canal Coy. had received powers to divert a stream running over the plaintiff's land for the purpose of feeding the canal.   They did so divert it from 1800 to 1853, during which time as the result of the diversion (see judgment of Cockburn, C. J., at p. 589) the natural channel of the stream became silted up.   In 1864 the defendants, a Railway Company, successors to the Canal Company, having no further need for the water of the brook, restored it to its natural channel, with the result that when a time of flood came the channel was no longer large enough to contain it and it overflowed the land of the plaintiff. But it was held by Cockburn, C. J., that the plaintiff had no right of action, on the ground that although the damage might in a sense be said to have been caused by the act of the defendants, that act was one which they had a right to perform : since they were not bound to continue to divert the water any longer than they had a mind.   In the argument *National Manure Coy. v. Donald*, 4 H. and N. 8, was quoted, and referred to in the judgment of Blackburn, J., on the question as to whether the plaintiff had acquired a right under the Prescription Act against the Canal Co. to have the stream diverted.   But that case would seem to show this at any rate, that when the Canal Company became a Railway Company their right to divert the stream came to an end, so that they might have been liable for not returning it to its original course.

Another matter worth noticing here, not that it would have actually destroyed the right, but because the effect of it would have been to prevent any advantage being gained by the acquisition of a prescriptive right, is as follows. It was contended under the Prescription Act, though not under the Common Law for a reason that will presently appear, that as in many cases until the right had been gained by user for the required period, every act which contributed towards establishing that user was a trespass, an action of trespass might be brought after the right had been acquired in respect of each of the acts of user before the right was acquired. If that had been so and the damage had been held to be the value of the right so acquired the effect would have been to make it only possible to acquire prescriptive rights at their value.

It will be observed that at Common Law no such contention could be raised. It was quite true that until the proper period of user was completed each act was a trespass, and subject to action. But so soon as the requisite period had expired the case was different. Quite apart from any retrospective effect of the acts, at Common Law every prescription rested upon a presumed grant. Acts of user then were nothing more than evidence of such grant. Until they had been persevered in for the proper period they were insufficient evidence, and therefore actionable, but so soon as the period was completed then they proved the antecedent grant, and each act was done in exercise of a grant lawfully made and was not, and never had been, a trespass.

Under the Prescription Act the case was different. Under that Act the right "now depends upon positive enactment, it is matter juris positivi, and does not require, and therefore ought not to be rested on, any presumption of grant;" per Lord Westbury in *Tapling v. Jones*, 11 H. L. C. 290.

That being so the intermediate acts, it was argued, must each of them at the time have been trespasses and the mere fact that by a series of wrongful acts a right was established under the Prescription Act at the termination of the series did not deprive the individual acts of their wrongful character. But it was held in *Wright v. Williams*, 1 M. and W. 77, that this was not so. As Lord Abinger, C. B., put the argument at p. 99. It was argued that the pleas were absurd, "for each justifies an act done at a particular time by the defendant as being *then* lawful and *then* done because the defendant actually enjoyed the right of doing the same thing for a period of time afterwards": so that it is said the character of the act, whether it be wrongful or rightful cannot be known at the time by the party doing it, but depends upon a subsequent event. But their view was this: "It appears to us that the statute in question intended to confer, after the periods of enjoyment therein mentioned, a right from their first commencement, and to legalize every act done in the exercise of the right during their continuance." And it will be remembered that *Barlow v. Ross,* 24 Q. B. D. 381, the case where it was held that compensation was payable for rights, not yet acquired, but in process of being acquired under the Prescription Act, is in affirmance of the principle that before the required period acts of user do give an inchoate right.

I have now completed my task so far as time has allowed me. I do not think I can more appropriately conclude than by quoting the words of the Real Property Commissioners in the first Report upon Prescription and Limitation.

"It might at first sight be considered that the duration of wrong ought not to give it a sanction, and that the long suffering of injury should be no bar to the obtaining of right when demanded. But human affairs must be conducted on other principles. It is found to be of the greatest importance, to promote peace, by affixing a period to the right of disturbing possession. Experience teaches us that owing to the perishable nature of all evidence, the truth cannot be ascertained on any contested question of fact after a considerable lapse of time. The temptation to introduce false evidence grows with the difficulty of detecting it; and, at last, long possession affords the proof, the most safely to be relied upon, of the right of property. Independently of the question of right, the disturbance of property after long enjoyment is mischievous. It is accordingly found both reasonable and useful that enjoyment for a certain period of time against all claimants should be considered conclusive evidence of title."

INDEX.